Seven
Wonders
for a
Cool Planet

Seven Wonders

for a

Cool Planet

Everyday Things to Help Solve Global Warming

Eric Sorensen

and the staff of SIGHTLINE INSTITUTE

SIERRA CLUB BOOKS
San Francisco

The Sierra Club, founded in 1892 by author and conservationist John Muir, is the oldest, largest, and most influential grassroots environmental organization in the United States. With more than a million members and supporters—and some sixty chapters across the country—we are working hard to protect our local communities, ensure an enduring legacy for America's wild places, and find smart energy solutions to stop global warming. To learn how you can participate in the Sierra Club's programs to explore, enjoy, and protect the planet, please address inquiries to Sierra Club, 85 Second Street, San Francisco, California 94105, or visit our website at www.sierraclub.org.

The Sierra Club's book publishing division, Sierra Club Books, has been a leading publisher of titles on the natural world and environmental issues for nearly half a century. We offer books to the general public as a nonprofit educational service in the hope that they may enlarge the public's understanding of the Sierra Club's concerns and priorities. The point of view expressed in each book, however, does not necessarily represent that of the Sierra Club. For more information on Sierra Club Books and a complete list of our titles and authors, please visit www.sierraclub.org/books.

Published by Sierra Club Books
85 Second Street, San Francisco, CA 94105

Sierra Club Books are published in association with
Counterpoint (www.counterpointpress.com).

Sierra Club, Sierra Club Books, and the Sierra Club design logos are registered trademarks of the Sierra Club.

Book and cover design by Linda Herman, Glyph Publishing Arts
Front cover photo of ceiling fan © Hunter Fans

Library of Congress Cataloging-in-Publication Data

Sorensen, Eric
   Seven wonders for a cool planet : everyday things to help solve global warming / Eric Sorensen and the staff of Sightline Institute.
       p. cm.
   ISBN 978-1-57805-145-8 (pbk.)
1. Global warming—Popular works. 2. Environmental protection—
Citizen participation. I. Sightline Institute. II. Title.
   QC981.8.G56S62 2008
   640—dc22   2008003871

Printed in the United States of America on New Leaf Ecobook 50 acid-free paper, which contains a minimum of 50 percent post-consumer waste, processed chlorine free. Of the balance, 25 percent is Forest Stewardship Council certified to contain no old-growth trees and to be pulped totally chlorine free.

Distributed to the trade by Publishers Group West
12 11 10 09 08
10 9 8 7 6 5 4 3 2 1

Contents

Acknowledgments

Seven Wonders for a Cool Planet is testament to the staying power of a good idea. It was adapted from a book created in 1999 by Sightline Institute (then Northwest Environment Watch) and published by Sierra Club Books: *Seven Wonders: Everyday Things for a Healthier Planet* by John C. Ryan. (That book grew out of an article written by Alan Durning called "The Seven Sustainable Wonders of the World," published in *Utne Reader* in 1994.) We are particularly indebted to Ryan, as the original author of the book, and we also thank the rest of the staff from that time, as well as the board, donors, funders, and volunteers who made the original *Seven Wonders* possible.

Seven Wonders for a Cool Planet* was adapted and rewritten by Eric Sorensen. Sightline staff members contributed additional research and writing, especially senior researcher Eric de Place, who managed the project; executive director Alan Durning; communications strategist Anna Fahey; communications director Elisa Murray; and research director Clark Williams-Derry. We also benefited enormously from volunteer research assistance by former Sightline interns Justin Brant, Jessica Branom-Zwick, Deric Gruen, and Matt Schoell-hamer. Without their dedication and generosity, this book would not have been written. And Sightline is extremely grateful to the rest of its hardworking staff, as well as to the many volunteers who donate their precious time and other resources to help us maximize our impact.

We are indebted—and very grateful—to our board of directors for their donation of much time and support; to our trustees and advisors; and to the community of faithful donors fueling our mission. They make projects like this one possible. We particularly wish to thank the members of the Cascadia Stewards Council, Sightline's society of major donors, for their strategic, foundational support.

We also thank Sierra Club Books for giving new life—and a climate twist—to an idea that hasn't gone out of style. We thank copyeditor Elizabeth Berg, acting editorial director Diana Landau, publisher Helen Sweet-land, and Sierra Club executive director Carl Pope.

Introduction

Racing Against the Clock

HERE'S AN UNLIKELY DUO of cultural icons: Jack Bauer and Pope Benedict XVI.

No, the ethically challenged hero of television's hit show *24* and the moral beacon of a billion people won't be sharing a podium any time soon. But they are of one mind on this century's most pressing concern: global warming.

The producers of *24* are using a biodiesel blend in the show's vehicles and generators, tapping renewable electricity sources, reducing their paper use, and even incorporating a climate-change theme into the show's plot. The Roman Catholic pontiff is getting around in an electric popemobile and pushing to make Vatican City the first sovereign state to go carbon neutral.

They're in good company. England's Prince Charles and the NFL's Super Bowl talk of being carbon neutral, reducing greenhouse-gas emissions where possible and canceling the rest with offsets or green-energy investments.

Al Gore's documentary about global warming has won him an Academy Award, and his long crusade to mobilize awareness on the topic earned him a share of the Nobel Peace Prize. Two billion people—nearly one-third of the planet—tuned in to a multicontinent pop music extravaganza for the cause.

After decades of scientific warnings, global warming has shot to the top of the political agenda. More significantly, this challenge has burst into the mainstream of public consciousness. We now understand that we are disrupting the planet's climate enough to jeopardize our cities, towns, and ecological underpinnings. Global warming profoundly affects human well-being, be it with deadly heat waves, crop failures, worsening storms, waning water supplies, or rising ocean levels. Many plants and animals also are finding their accustomed habitats uninhabitable. You've seen the movie: Calving icebergs. Starving polar bears. Wildfires. Katrina. While other factors are in play, there's broad agreement that human-caused climate change is raising the stakes on such "natural" disasters.

It's taken a while to get here. The earliest intimations of the global-warming problem go back to the 1820s, when French polymath Joseph Fourier discovered that atmospheric gases increased the earth's temperature—

the greenhouse effect. A full century has passed since Swedish chemist Svante Arrhenius speculated that increasing amounts of carbon dioxide in the atmosphere could cause the earth to warm, and half a century has gone by since American oceanographer Roger Revelle linked global warming to fossil-fuel use and predicted that we might be seeing its effects by the new millennium.

But by now, the human impact on climate has been established many times over by worldwide scientific consensus. The Nobel Committee awarded the Nobel Peace Prize not only to Gore but to the Intergovernmental Panel on Climate Change scientists, which forged agreement on the link between human activity and global warming. Hardly a week goes by without someone pointing out a new climate-related wrinkle or proposing measures to address the problem.

The challenge we face has been compared to World War II, the civil rights movement, and the global fight against infectious disease, but it may well be more comprehensive than any of these struggles. Tackling it will require one of the most unified efforts in the history of civilization. Old technologies will need to be used in new ways; whole new technologies will need to be invented and adopted. New political alliances and agreements will need to be forged and implemented. Work is already under way to create economic incentives, whether it's a global-warming tax or a cap-and-trade system, to encourage more clean energy and discourage greenhouse pollution. Hundreds of U.S. cities have pledged climate reductions; three blocs of North American states and provinces have banded together to jointly reduce emissions; and every developed nation in the world (save the United States and Australia) has given the Kyoto Protocol the force of law. And that's only the tip of the melting iceberg. Many of the world's biggest corporations have stepped up to call for climate protection, realizing the economic opportunities in being part of the transition to a clean-energy-powered economy, and the economic dangers of doing nothing.

We've identified the key steps needed to arrest climate change—improving energy efficiency, using less carbon-intensive power and fuel, and storing excess carbon in trees and soil (and possibly deep underground). Much of the power to take these steps lies in the hands of policy makers, engineers, and the energy industry. But while political leaders and institutions are coming to grips with climate disruption, millions of individuals are doing what they can in their own way.

With the help of online carbon calculators, people are tallying the impressive amounts of the invisible gases that flow so insidiously from our everyday devices. The typical clothes washer, hot water included, cranks out the equivalent of 1,544 pounds of carbon dioxide and other greenhouse gases a year. That's the weight of a rodeo bull. According to research by energy analyst Rick Heede, your clothes dryer is responsible for almost as much.

Your home computer produces more than six times its weight in carbon each year. Your telephone answering machine, if you still have one, requires 51 pounds of carbon dioxide a year, the same as your cordless telephone and only a little more than your color television— when it is off. Then there's a bevy of fuel burners like lawnmowers and boat motors and the daddy of them all, the big kahuna: the automobile.

We have a lot to do. Chances are you've already heard the litany of ways to reduce your carbon footprint: Turn down the hot water heater. Drop the thermostat two degrees in winter and raise it three in summer. Wash your clothes in cold water. Caulk and insulate. Use compact fluorescent bulbs. Inflate your car tires. The Internet is crawling with tips—hundreds of them.

Seven Wonders for a Cool Planet is not another book of tips. Like its antecedents in the "seven wonders of the world" lineage, it's a guide to miraculous human-made things. The twist about these wonders is that they already surround you. This book is an ode to seven everyday devices you probably already own or use, which are so powerful, elegant, and in most cases simple, that they are and always have been friends of the climate (and also of your pocketbook, neighbors, health, and children). It's a reminder of everything that's right about our lives, not everything that's wrong.

More subversively, *Seven Wonders* is a way to think— illustrated seven ways—about solving the climate crisis once and for all: by designing sustainability into the very heart of our lives, communities, institutions, and economy.

It's a way to reimagine the problem, starting with a few mostly low-tech tools and notions. Each of the seven wonders carries the weight of a larger idea, a more encompassing way to see the global-warming challenge and its solutions. Yes, a *bicycle* really can fight global warming all by itself, with every bike trip reducing the five tons of carbon dioxide a year that an average car cranks out. And when we consider its wondrous simplicity, we can more clearly see the Faustian bargain of a transportation system built around the car, source of about one-third of our global-warming pollution. We see that cars have not only damaged the climate but also have harmed our health, clogged our cities, and spawned suburbs whose residents often have no option but to live by the gas pedal. Now even those errands we could do without motorization are too often done by car. A bicycle can help break that habit, and it can get us to think about the larger task at hand—reorienting our communities so that more of us can get around without resorting to internal combustion. It's healthier for us and for the atmosphere too.

Consider how the other half-dozen cool planet wonders fight global warming and expand how we think about it. Ounce for ounce, the *condom* may have helped give more pleasure—and prevented more global warming—than any device going. On average, condoms are used nearly a million times a day in America. Presumably that's two million people having a pretty good time. It's also a lot of pregnancies prevented and lot of people who have not contracted HIV/AIDS or other diseases. Moreover, the condom gives couples a hand in slowing population growth. The United States is a world leader in both unintended pregnancies and per capita carbon emissions. The little old condom can help bring both under control.

The *ceiling fan*—which is already installed in 65 million American homes—uses far less energy than an air-conditioning unit, and makes air conditioning cool better. But it's generally overlooked as the American obsession with temperature control has reshaped our architecture and transformed whole cities. Energy efficiency, on the other hand, lets us turn ideas into kilowatts. With smart designs, better technology, and tools as inspired as a ceiling fan or a programmable thermostat, we can keep cooling our bodies, heating our water, and lighting our homes—and put a lot less carbon into the air.

For those too young to remember, a *clothesline* is a piece of rope that Americans once strung outdoors to dry clothes. You can still buy one for about ten dollars. And talk about a great gift idea: the clothesline keeps on giving in the form of lower energy bills, while, just like other kinds of renewable energy, the free solar power that dries your shirt on the line never runs out.

And what about the local *real tomato*, which marries fuel efficiency and peak taste? Fossil fuels go into fertilizers, farm equipment, and the tractor trailers that move our fruits and vegetables and cereal and bottled water and boneless chicken breast thousands of miles. Simply by looking at two tomatoes—the pale red hardball sold in a supermarket and the real tomato found in a farmer's market—you can see how locally grown food and other sustainable food options taste superior. Better yet, they can improve our food mileage and contribute to a low-carbon diet.

A host of things that we bring into our home have a high, often hidden, carbon price tag. The **library book** is not one of them. The book you borrow is the book that doesn't require extra cutting of carbon-saving trees. Other reused items and materials have an equally powerful impact on conserving resources and curbing the massive amounts of carbon produced by manufacturing. Your local video store is full of them. So is your thrift store. And eBay. And Craigslist.

The **microchip** is taking the library model one step further, revolutionizing the way we deliver and manage words and data to the point that some books and other materials, like bricks and mortar, are becoming obsolete. The digital systems that microchips inhabit are helping us cut down on commuting, making warehouses irrelevant, and creating an economy built around information more than around fuel-consuming stuff.

The benefits of our seven wonders don't flow just to the climate. They benefit the people who use them, and in a range of ways. Half the trips you take by car can be taken almost as quickly (or quicker) by bike while you get fit and save money on gas. And talk about energy efficient: Every mile traveled by bike rather than by car keeps a pound of carbon dioxide out of the atmosphere, while reducing cash-draining stops at the pump. Checking out books from the library instead of buying them saves on both carbon dioxide and money—far more than the twenty dollars or so you pay each year in taxes to support libraries.

For the many of us who are eager to rise to the challenge of global warming, the seven wonders provide a convenient handle. We see the problem. We know that our leaders need to do something, and soon. But we need to know that each of us can play a part. So while the pope is going solar and Jack Bauer takes a break from saving the planet to . . . well, save the planet, aficionados of the seven wonders can ride bikes, hang clothes, "don johnnies," and telecommute. Ultimately, the seven wonders help us do much more. They inspire us to think differently—to find new ways to make our familiar tools help us save energy and money on heating systems, computers, unused lights, and phantom appliances that suck energy even when we think they are off. They show us that doing the right thing is no sacrifice; on the contrary, it's financially and emotionally rewarding.

Each of us in our own way can adapt the seven wonders to our greatest benefit. We won't have the power of a shadowy agency behind us, like Jack Bauer, or the vast following (and wealth) of the Vatican, but we have unlimited strength in numbers and the endlessly renewable resource of human ingenuity. With these we can retool everyday things to escape the toughest of predicaments.

⟦ *The Bicycle* ⟧

A FRIEND TELLS this tale of woe:

"I remember the morning clearly. I left the house by the back door, keys in hand, ready to slide onto the driver's seat and head down the driveway to work. But there was just an empty space where I had left my vehicle. I couldn't comprehend for a second: did I park somewhere else last night? Then it dawned on me: my Cannondale eighteen-speed bicycle, my traveling companion for nearly a decade, had been stolen.

"It's silly to get so attached to a piece of aluminum and steel, but having my bicycle stolen from my own back porch felt almost like losing a limb. For nine years, that bike had been my almost daily companion, even part of my identity." He even wondered if his bicycle relationship had become unhealthy, too close. He could see himself on an *Oprah* episode: "Men Who Love Their Vehicles Too Much."

But there's nothing strange about loving a bike: people and bicycles were made for each other. The bicycle is a wonder of physics. It harnesses human muscle power directly to that old-time marvel—the wheel—and yields a vehicle more energy-efficient than any other devised, ever, by anyone. A human on a bicycle is more efficient (in calories expended per pound and per mile) than a train, truck, airplane, boat, automobile, motorcycle, skateboard, canoe, or jet pack. Not only that, bicycling is more efficient than walking, which takes three times as many calories per mile. In fact, pound for pound, a person on a bike can go farther on a calorie of food than a gazelle can running, a salmon swimming, or an eagle flying. That's impressive!

Thanks to these awesome physics, the bicycle costs pennies per mile and less than bus fare per trip. It emits no greenhouse gases, local pollutants, or engine noise. It provides moderate, low-impact exercise of the kind the human body needs in abundance to maintain health and vitality. Oh, and it is hugely democratic: it is equally available to all. That's why on the highways, byways, and bikeways in most of the world, cycling is the transportation mainstream.

The bicycle is the world's most ubiquitous transport vehicle. Bicycles outnumber automobiles almost two to one worldwide, and their production outpaces cars by three to one. Rush-hour traffic in China is dominated by human-powered vehicles; even in the wealthy cities of Europe and Japan, a large share of the populace gets around by bike.

Only in North America is it still treated as little more than a plaything. About 50 million American adults (and 40 million children) ride their bikes at least once each year, but only about 2 million are regular bike commuters. Of all trips in the United States, just two-thirds of one percent are made by bicycle. Similarly, only 1 percent of Canadian commuters report bicycling as their usual mode of transportation. Some government agencies have embraced bikes, but they remain the exception. The reports from Canada's national transportation agency rarely mention bicyclists, except as victims of traffic accidents.

A bike is a blessing for your wallet, health, and legs, but bicycles are sustainable wonders because of what they *don't* do to the world. At zero pounds of carbon dioxide emissions a day, versus the car's one pound per mile, a bike does not alter the global climate. A bicyclist fuels up on carbohydrates, not fossil fuels and imported oil. Bicycles don't cause traffic jams or require paving over whole landscapes at the expense of croplands, government coffers, and livable neighborhoods. And bicycles are not the leading killer of Americans and Canadians two to twenty-four years old or, worldwide, of men fifteen to forty-four years old. That distinction is reserved for the automobile.

An amazing invention, the automobile has given humans unprecedented mobility. Yet cars have proliferated to the detriment of all other means of getting around and at great expense to human and natural communities. Today, Americans make 85 percent of all trips by car. "Two cars in the garage" no longer suffices as the American Dream: one in five American households now owns three vehicles or more. Cars so dominate transportation systems and communities in North America that their own usefulness is on the wane: they are crowding themselves to a standstill.

The American love affair with the automobile is also a prime culprit in the nation's outsized carbon footprint. On average, each of the world's residents produces 8,800 pounds of carbon dioxide a year. But Americans on average produce nearly five times as much CO_2, with an average of 11,350 pounds a year coming from each American passenger car.

If Americans replaced just one in five of their average-length car trips by bicycling, each driver would spare the atmosphere more than one ton of carbon dioxide emissions each year. Collectively, the effect would be comparable to taking 48 million vehicles off the road—as if everyone in both California and New York State stopped driving.

Cars crank out the CO_2 in other ways, too, starting with how they get made. Roughly 11 percent of the total CO_2 emitted over the full life cycle of a car can be traced to its manufacture. The roads it rides on are big carbon producers as well. For each mile of new lane, the materials and machinery used to build a highway release between 1,400 and 2,300 tons of greenhouse gases. As much if not more fossil-fuel energy is then used to maintain the highway. An Australian study estimated that forty years of road maintenance requires more than three times as much energy as it did to build the road to begin with.

Transportation is currently so dependent on fossil fuels that the transportation sector (cars, trucks, planes, boats, and trains) accounted for one-third of all U.S. energy-related carbon dioxide emissions in 2005. Motor gasoline represented 60 percent of total transportation sector emissions, or about 20 percent of all energy-related emissions in the United States. Bottom line: if you want to do one thing to reduce your carbon footprint, step away from the car.

The American Dream of cars in every garage is an impossible dream for the world as a whole. Even ignoring the climate toll, the economic costs alone prohibit the dream's coming true. Fewer than 10 percent of humans can afford to buy a car, while roughly 80 percent of humans can afford to buy a bicycle. Building the necessary roads and parking spaces would bankrupt governments and probably threaten world food supplies. China, for example, would have to pave the equivalent of 40 percent of the nation's cropland to give each of its citizens access to as much pavement as an American has.

Activists, engineers, and planners are working hard to promote alternatives to our problematic car-dominated system. Buses, trains, and carpools produce less pollution and traffic than does solo driving—but lack the privacy and door-to-door convenience of cars. Vehicles powered by alternative fuels or electricity (including hybrids), as well as proposed "hypercars" able to cross the continent on a tank of gas, could minimize cars' greenhouse-gas emissions. But even such cars do nothing about the problems of traffic, sprawl, or deadly accidents. Though a variety of choices is key to reforming our car-centered transportation system, the only vehicle that addresses all the environmental liabilities of cars—particularly their climate contribution—is the bicycle.

Bicycles are not for everyone, and they're not for every trip. Cars do many things that bicycles cannot easily do: carry heavy loads uphill, protect riders from the elements, and cover long distances quickly. But a surprising number of car trips could easily be made by bike. Nearly half of all trips in the United States are three miles or less; more than a quarter are less than a mile. While advertising sells cars and trucks as tools for the open road, most often they help us inhabit a small daily realm—"Errandsville"—defined by home, store, job, and school. Many of these trips are easily bikable— or walkable—even on roads designed without bicycles or pedestrians in mind. A bicyclist can easily cover a mile in four minutes, while a pedestrian requires just fifteen.

Short car trips are, naturally, the easiest to replace with a bike trip (or even walking). Mile for mile, they are also the most polluting. Engines running cold, at typical urban speeds, produce four times the carbon monoxide and twice the volatile organic compounds (VOCs) as engines running hot. And at the end of a trip, smog-forming (and carcinogenic) VOCs continue to evaporate from an engine until it cools off, whether the engine's been running for five minutes or five hours.

Many more of these short trips would be made under human power if bike-friendly amenities like bike lanes, bike traffic signals, and secure bike parking were common. Nearly half of recreational riders in the United States—or one out of five of all adults—say they would sometimes bike to work if better bike lanes or paths existed. But not even half of one percent of U.S. commuters arrive at work by bicycle on any given day. Among major U.S. cities, those with extensive bicycle lanes have three times the rate of bike commuting compared to other cities.

We can act as individuals by choosing to ride a bike whenever it's possible and by being safely equipped and attentive to road hazards. But there's only so much an individual can do. Collective action through government is essential to provide safer and more appealing places to ride. Policies from local zoning laws to federal highway funding and tax codes favor driving over all other modes of transport; revised policies can just as effectively do the reverse. In the California cities of Davis and Palo Alto, crisscrossed with bike lanes, at least one out of five trips is made by bicycle. In Japan, which has a similar rate of bicycle ownership but higher gasoline taxes and more restrictive parking than the United States, one out of six workers relies on a bicycle for the daily commute.

Bike-friendly policies, from traffic calming to car-free downtown zones, have boosted cycling rates in five European nations to 10 percent or more of urban trips; one-fifth of all trips in Danish cities are made by bike, and one-third in Dutch cities. By slowing down cars, traffic-calming measures like street-narrowing curb bulbs and traffic diverters at intersections make streets safer and more pleasant for everyone—not just bikers.

Ours is a car culture, but it's easy to forget that one out of three people in both the United States and Canada cannot drive. Children, the elderly, the disabled, and those who cannot afford to drive are often stranded by our transportation system. Compact cities with safe and pleasant streetscapes benefit not only people who want to choose their desired mode of transportation but also those for whom driving is not an option. A surprising number of nondrivers could be bikers, given half a chance: in Europe's compact and bikable cities, many senior citizens bicycle, helping them maintain vitality and prolong active, independent lives. In large cities in China, 20 percent of people over sixty bicycle as their primary mode of transportation.

The Bicycle

Taxpayers and budget cutters are other constituencies that should support bicycling. Conditions for bicyclists can be improved cheaply and quickly: often it takes only a bucket of paint to make a bike lane or shave unneeded width off a car lane. Other programs—like building bike paths or installing bike racks—are more expensive but still cheaper than similar investments for cars because bikes require so little space to use and park. It costs as much as twenty times more to support a passenger-mile of automobile traffic compared to one of bicycle traffic.

Bicycles are a far cheaper way of providing mobility for the masses, but in the end it's not mobility that people really want; it's access. When destinations are closer, people can do the things they want to do while expending less time and energy in travel. And compact urban form encourages alternative modes of travel: more trips are within walking or biking range, and mass transit becomes more cost-effective with more riders per area. In the long run, the measures most crucial to getting more people on their feet and on their bikes are those that fight sprawl and encourage dense, livable cities. On average, city dwellers drive a third as much— and half as fast—as suburbanites. To legalize and encourage the mixing of homes, shops, and offices, local zoning codes can be revised. And tax codes and land-use regulations can reward builders who fill in the underused space in existing cities and towns, not those who turn farm and forest land into "Foxmeadow Farms" subdivisions and "Cedar Knolls" business parks.

Biking has made progress in North America in recent years. Many localities and a few states have begun to redesign their streets to better accommodate cyclists and pedestrians. In the United States, federal transportation funding for biking and walking has risen from $6 million in 1990 to $422 million in 2003. Since 1994, state-level staff committed to working on bicycle and pedestrian issues has roughly doubled, and twenty-nine of the fifty states have adopted statewide bicycle or bicycle and pedestrian plans.

Sportworks, a manufacturer of bike racks for buses, has customers in all fifty states, with more than five hundred agencies and municipalities using their equipment. The company estimates its racks are used more than one million times a month. Nearly half the United States' 12,656 local police departments are using bicycles, lending further respectability to bikes as effective tools for mobility.

Perhaps the most important pro-bicycle milestone in North America was the passage of ISTEA by the U.S. Congress in 1991. Under ISTEA (short for . . . never mind; just call it "ice tea" like everyone else), 1 percent of federal transportation funding has supported projects improving conditions for pedestrians and cyclists. ISTEA created bike and pedestrian coordinator positions in every state and funded bike lanes, bike racks, and other facilities around the nation. SAFETEA, passed in 2003, continues federal funding of bicycle and pedestrian projects, as well as providing $500,000 for bike safety education.

Yet these measures pale when compared with those in nations that make bicycling a priority: the Netherlands, for example, spends 10 percent of its roads budget to support bicycle facilities. For the moment, most city and suburban streets in North America remain inhospitable to anyone who is not in a car, and sprawl still rules the day. Imagine trying to walk or bike a mile in any direction from a shopping mall near your home. Then think instead about making your next shopping trip somewhere you can walk or bike home from.

A bicycle is radically different from a car in its simplicity, power source, and climate impact: the idea that bikes can do many of the jobs that cars now do may take some getting used to. But thinking differently is the only way to do more than fiddle at the margins of the world's burning challenges. After all, we in the industrial world need to reduce our greenhouse-gas emissions by some 90 percent to avoid the worst dangers of climate disruption.

To prevent many more species and ecosystems from going extinct, we need to have less habitat covered or fragmented by roads, suburbs, and other human artifacts. An ever-increasing fleet of cars—no matter how clean their tailpipes—on ever-spreading grids of pavement is simply not compatible with these goals. But along with compact communities that foster foot power and bus travel, bicycles can take us where we need to go—at a fraction of the climate and economic cost produced by cars.

British author H. G. Wells may have summed it up best more than a half-century ago: "When I see an adult on a bicycle, I do not despair for the future of the human race."

[*The Condom*]

TODAY, HUMAN BEINGS WILL HAVE SEX more than 100 million times. For many millions of couples, all this lovemaking will bring great pleasure, yet at least 350,000 people will catch a painful disease from their partners. Today's sex will also make one million women around the world pregnant—about half of them unintentionally.

On this day, one simple object invented centuries ago will spare thousands, if not millions, of people from life-threatening diseases and unwanted pregnancies: the condom. Though not the most widely used method of contraception, the condom is the only one (short of abstinence) that effectively prevents the spread of diseases like chlamydia, gonorrhea, and AIDS. Perhaps one in six of today's acts of sexual intercourse will involve a condom.

The condom is a remarkable little device. It weighs in at a fraction of an ounce, and can be as thin as $\frac{1}{500}$ of an inch, yet it simultaneously fights three of the most serious problems facing humans at the beginning of the twenty-first century: sexually transmitted diseases (STDs), unwanted pregnancies, and population growth. Those last two can have an outsize effect on climate change. With just a modest decrease in unintended pregnancies, we can go a long way toward slowing the world's population growth and the carbon dioxide emissions that inevitably follow in each person's wake—especially the wake of North Americans. All thanks to the wonders of a flimsy elastic tube.

Though it often provokes humor or embarrassment, the party hat is widely appreciated for all the good it does. Primarily in response to the spread of AIDS, condom sales grew rapidly in the 1980s. Sales have fallen off since the 1990s, but the market research firm A. C. Nielsen estimates Americans still bought 354 million prophylactics in 2002. The U.S. Agency for International Development ships an even greater number overseas. Once sold mostly from behind pharmacy counters, condoms are found today in supermarkets, convenience stores, warehouse clubs, catalogs, and countless web outlets. In much of the world, using condoms has become a norm of responsible sexuality.

A fraction of an ounce of responsibility can go a long way in helping the health of the planet and of the people that inhabit it. Researchers theorize that just a 14 percent increase in the use of contraceptives can lead to a decrease of one child per woman in the total fertility rate, the average number of children who would be born to a woman in her lifetime. This could translate into 1 billion fewer births by the middle of this century, with dramatically less carbon dioxide being emitted. Based on today's emission rates, a billion fewer humans might spare the planet perhaps 4 billion tons of carbon dioxide emissions each year.

The effect would be particularly dramatic in the United States, world leader in the production of global-warming gases. If the average North American life expectancy holds at seventy-eight years, each person can expect to produce 1,630 tons of carbon dioxide over his or her lifetime.

Inadequate contraception is not just a Third World issue, as some people think. The United States has a much higher rate of unintended pregnancy than most other developed nations—higher even than dozens of developing nations. Roughly half of all U.S. pregnancies are unintended. And a baby born in North America will use roughly twenty-five times more resources over the course of its life than a baby born in the developing world.

While the populations of many European nations are stable or shrinking slightly, the population of the United States has expanded since 2000 by 1 percent—the equivalent of adding a Kansas every year. Natural increase (births minus deaths) is responsible for two-thirds of the growth, immigration the rest. Canada is also expanding by about 1 percent annually—the equivalent of a Nova Scotia every three years—but with slightly less than half its growth due to natural increase. Immigration has local impacts but, of course, does not add to the total number of people on the Earth, now rising by about 75 million people each year.

The condom is a wonder that's not only good for the climate but manifestly good for people too. AIDS is a global epidemic that now rivals history's worst, and despite the development of new drug treatments, the epidemic is far from over. In 2006, nearly 3 million people died of AIDS and another 39.5 million people were living with the disease. In Latin America and the Caribbean, AIDS has overtaken traffic injuries as a cause of death. In ten sub-Saharan countries, more than one in every ten adults was infected with the virus in the 1990s. Average life expectancy in Botswana, where one in four adults is infected, decreased from sixty-five to forty-five between 1990 and

2005. In the Caribbean, AIDS is the leading cause of death between the ages of fifteen and forty-four.

Even in North America, where health care is better and many AIDS victims can afford expensive antiviral "drug cocktails," the disease remains a major killer. In 2004, HIV was the sixth largest cause of death among Americans ages twenty-five to forty-four. And as of 2007, AIDS was twice as common per capita in the United States as in Canada. In both nations, minority groups such as blacks, Hispanics, and indigenous people lack access to quality health care and contract the disease at much higher rates.

And AIDS is only the tip of the condom, so to speak, of sexually transmitted disease. Unsafe sex is also spreading a range of curable but often deadly ailments (trichomoniasis, chlamydia, gonorrhea, hepatitis, and syphilis among them) to nearly 400 million victims, including 14 million North Americans each year. STDs can kill in many ways. Because of the lesions and inflammation they cause, they greatly increase the odds of catching HIV during sex. They also lead to infertility, miscarriages, and stillbirths, as well as pneumonia in newborn infants. STDs are the world's leading cause of cervical cancer, and they can lead to fatal hemorrhages during childbirth.

Unwanted pregnancies fuel population growth and all the associated ecological harm, but their toll is heaviest among women. One woman dies each minute because of complications during pregnancy, childbirth, or unsafe abortion. As Mahmoud Fathalla of the World Health Organization observed, "Without fertility regulation, women's rights are mere words. A woman who has no control over her fertility cannot complete her education, cannot maintain gainful employment . . . and has very few real choices open to her."

Contraceptive use has risen in recent years, and population growth slowed, as women's social and economic status has improved in many nations. Yet contraceptives—especially condoms—need to become much more widely used. By a rough estimate, lovers will employ condoms in only about half of today's 40 million or so acts of sexual intercourse worldwide that risk unwanted pregnancy or disease. One survey of Americans with multiple sex partners revealed that those who never use condoms, or use them inconsistently, outnumber those who always "rip and roll" by eleven to one. Canadian surveys suggest that as many as half of Canadians with multiple sex partners do not "dress appropriately" every time they have sex.

A key step is to make contraceptives universally available. Perhaps 500 million couples around the world wish to avoid or delay pregnancy but lack the means to do so. In fact, U.S. federal funding for international family planning programs declined by more than 30 percent between 1995 and 2005. Family planning inside the United States has also received reduced government funding over the past decade. This is particularly hard on low-income women who lack insurance, and has been linked to a 29 percent rise in unintended pregnancies. In 2000, the Equal Employment Opportunity Commission (EEOC) ruled that employers may not discriminate against women in their health insurance plans by denying benefits for prescription contraceptives if they have prescription drug benefits. Moreover, twenty-six states have laws mandating that contraception be covered by private insurance. Still, not all private insurance companies cover birth control other than sterilization. Similarly, many U.S. insurance companies will pay for Viagra to help a man have sex, but none pay for condoms to enable him to have sex safely.

For family planning and reproductive health services to be effective, they need to offer women and couples choices among a variety of contraceptive methods.

Condoms lack the side effects of birth-control pills and IUDs and the irreversibility of sterilization, but they have a higher failure rate than these other contraceptives. As many as one in six women becomes pregnant during her first year of sex using condoms, but this high rate is due to sporadic—or improper—use. One out of five British men asked to put a condom on a model penis failed to do it right: they tried to unroll the "johnnie" from the inside out. The most important way to improve condoms' effectiveness is to teach people how to use them properly, especially how to avoid spills and tears. With proper and consistent use, condoms' failure rate drops to 2 percent or less of women getting pregnant during their first year of use.

Contraceptive misuse and unintended pregnancies are more frequent in the United States than in other developed nations in part because talk of sex is still taboo in most schools even as it saturates pop culture. Only 10 percent of U.S. students receive comprehensive sex education; one out of four U.S. school districts has an abstinence-only curriculum. Through both direct funding and matching grants, the U.S. government steered some $1.5 billion to abstinence-only education programs between 1996 and 2006.

The Condom

Abstinence is the most effective form of contraception and prevention of sexually transmitted diseases. But try telling that to the roughly 200 million people worldwide having sex on any given day.

The condom is the only cool-planet wonder designed to be thrown away after one use. Fortunately, because almost all condoms are made from natural latex (rubber), their ecological impact is much lower than if they were made from synthetic rubber. For example, it takes at least three tons of petroleum to make a ton of synthetic rubber. Synthetic rubber also lacks natural latex's great strength and elasticity, essential qualities for condoms. (And airplane tires, for that matter. All the world's commercial airplanes and even the space shuttle roll on tires made of processed tree sap.)

And whatever impacts rubber production has, condoms are responsible for exceedingly little of it. The natural rubber in one car tire is enough to make 1,100 condoms.

Condom packaging does leave much to be desired. A highly (ahem) scientific survey conducted in aisle 8B of Bartell's Drugs in downtown Seattle revealed that just one of twenty-seven types of condoms for sale came in

Where the Rubber Meets the Air

The lowly tire gets less attention than flashy hybrids or theoretical hydrogen cars in the quest to slash emissions. But from rubber harvesting and transport to manufacture to on-road use to disposal, tires are prime candidates for cleaning up the atmosphere. Producing more than a billion annually, the tire industry is the biggest consumer of natural rubber, though synthetic rubber is also used in most tires.

The tires you buy, and how they are made, also vary in climate impact. In promoting fuel efficiency, tire makers tend to focus on "rolling resistance"—the energy needed to propel a car forward as the tires flex and deform to grip the road. Low-rolling-resistance tires can boost fuel efficiency by 1.5 to 4.5 percent. And whatever kind of tires you have, it's important to keep them properly inflated: an average driver will save about a tank of gas per year and stay safer, too. Systems that monitor tire pressure also help, especially in trucks.

The recycling market is big these days, with old tires being reduced to rubber "crumb" for various reuses. One environmentally friendly process uses vacuum distillation at low temperatures, preserving tire components and satisfying emissions standards. However recycling is done, it's a big step from burning old tires, one of the most toxic disposal methods imaginable.

health problems. Generating electricity accounts for 40 percent of U.S. energy-related carbon dioxide emissions. Roughly half of North America's electricity comes from burning coal, the dirtiest fossil fuel and the source of more than two out of every five tons of the carbon dioxide going into our air. According to the Rocky Mountain Institute, air-conditioning an average U.S. household sends about three tons of carbon dioxide up power plant smokestacks each year. Cold comfort indeed.

Unfortunately, more and more people are getting chills. U.S. exports of HVAC (heating, ventilating, and air-conditioning) equipment doubled between 2001 and 2005, and air-conditioner ownership in China recently tripled in just seven years. Many movie theaters and taxicabs in Indonesia are so cold they feel like meat lockers, reports a well-traveled friend. The booming tropical market for air-conditioning is doubly harmful: although production of ozone-depleting chlorofluoro-carbons (CFCs) has been banned in industrial nations since 1996, air conditioners and refrigerators sold in developing nations still contain CFCs (and will until 2010). CFC concentrations—and ozone holes—in the atmosphere peaked at the end of the twentieth century and today are slowly declining, yet the ozone layer won't fully repair itself until the twenty-second century.

Everyone deserves to be comfortable. But comfort doesn't have to mean the skinny range of temperatures many of us insist on. And it doesn't have to come at nearly the climate cost it does today. That's why the ceiling fan is a cool-planet wonder: it's an elegant and energy-efficient alternative to air-conditioning and all the problems air-conditioning causes.

Fans cool by creating light breezes that evaporate moisture from the skin. The gentle air circulation from a ceiling fan makes a room as comfortable as one where motionless air is 9°F (5°C) colder. Fans also work their wonders with very little electricity: at the highest speed, a typical ceiling fan uses fifty to seventy-five watts—as much as one incandescent light bulb and less than one-tenth the wattage of a medium-sized room air-conditioner. At the average U.S. price of electricity, running an average fan at its highest speed for twelve hours a day costs about three dollars a month; running the most efficient Energy Star–rated air conditioner would cost twenty-five dollars or more.

Much of the time, a ceiling fan will be enough for keeping cool. Even when it's not, using a fan with an air-conditioner can greatly increase efficiency while reducing the expense and impact of chilling the air. With a fan going, you can set a thermostat 9°F (5°C) higher and feel just as comfortable—and save about a third off your cooling (and global-warming) bill. (Each degree Fahrenheit you turn up the thermostat saves roughly 3 to 5 percent on air-conditioning costs.)

"Energy efficiency isn't just a free lunch," observes Amory Lovins of the Rocky Mountain Institute. "It's a lunch you are paid to eat."

Even before electricity was discovered, people cooled their homes effectively. For thousands of years, people designed their buildings to stay cool with thick, slow-to-heat walls, well-placed windows and vents, and other clever innovations. Temperatures in twelfth-century Anasazi pueblos, for example, varied only one-fourth as much as the harsh desert conditions outside their thick adobe walls. Environmentally attuned building design, in tandem with other energy efficiency measures, can reduce or eliminate the need for air-conditioning, even in extreme climates. An experimental (but normal-looking) tract house commissioned by Pacific Gas and Electric Company in Davis, California—where summer temperatures reach 110°F (43°C)—achieves standard comfort levels without an air conditioner. Because of good design and materials, including well-positioned and superinsulated windows, a light-colored roof, and efficient appliances, the family living there pays 80 percent less in energy bills than the neighbors do.

Air-conditioning is only one of many areas where we pay far too high a price—in dollars and pollution—because we let energy go to waste. Practically everything that we use energy for—cooling, heating, lighting, transporting, communicating, manufacturing, you name it—can be accomplished as well or better with much less energy. In *Factor Four: Doubling Wealth, Halving Resource Use*, Ernst von Weizsäcker of Germany's Wuppertal Institute and Amory and Hunter Lovins provide fifty examples where energy and material inputs can be profitably cut by at least a factor of four (75 percent) with no sacrifice in what the inputs were being used for. Reforms of such magnitude befit global ecological problems and forward-looking companies have been getting on board. Blue-chip corporations such as IBM, Wal-Mart, and DuPont are making serious pledges to boost efficiency, a move that should benefit both the global climate and their bottom line.

Multiplying energy efficiency is key to saving the world's climate. It may also be the only hope for most developing nations to achieve a decent level of prosperity in a world of limited—and increasingly degraded—resources. The whole world can have comfortable, well-lit indoor spaces, hot water, chilled foods, and other conveniences of modern life—but we can't afford the leaky buildings, poorly designed appliances, and harmful power plants that usually go with them. With energy used efficiently, there's no need for anyone to go through it as fast as the average North American does: nearly six times faster than the global average.

Buildings are a good place to start improving energy efficiency: they use a third of the energy and two-thirds of the electricity in the United States, the world's biggest energy consumer. Because power plants typically convert 40 percent or less of the energy in the fuel they burn to electricity (the rest is sent up a smoke-stack or down a drainpipe as waste heat), electricity saved in a home or business can save two to three times as much energy behind the scenes. And making lights and appliances more efficient saves energy twice over: reducing the waste heat they generate reduces room-cooling needs as well.

From skylights and ceiling fans to basement insulation, there are hundreds of ways to conserve energy in any given building. Many local utilities provide free or discounted energy audits to help businesses and home-owners determine their energy-saving priorities. All kinds of efficiency improvements can be made at a

No Wonder: Halogen Lamps

Lighting consumes roughly one-fifth of all U.S. electricity—one-fourth if you include the air-conditioning energy used to counteract the heat generated by the lights. As Amory Lovins of the Rocky Mountain Institute writes, incandescent lamps "are actually electric heaters that happen to emit 10 percent of their energy as light." Halogen lights, despite their longer lifespan, are also very inefficient: basically 700°F (400°C) heaters that emit 5 percent of their energy as light.

Halogen floor lamps are a prime offender; the 40 million or so of them operating in the United States use five times more power annually than is generated by wind and solar power combined. Safety concerns may help curtail their use, as they've been implicated in hundreds of fires and are banned at many colleges.

Both halogen and incandescent bulbs are easily replaced by compact fluorescent lamps—which can use one-third the electricity of halogen equivalents—to the benefit of the world's climate. Newer CFLs come in a wide color spectrum, and some are even dimmable. Some utilities, such as Pacific Gas & Electric, are giving them away as part of efforts to conserve energy. And a promising light on the horizon is the potential of LEDs to compete with CFLs in efficiency and lifespan; cost currently limits their use.

profit, but institutional barriers, as well as habit and backward economic incentives, wed our economy to its wasteful ways. With energy still relatively cheap in North America—highly subsidized and not held accountable for the costly damages it causes—too few people bother to conserve it. Green taxes on energy, matched with tax cuts on our paychecks or purchases, would reverse those incentives and give individuals and businesses more reason to improve the energy efficiency of everything from their washing machines to their factories. A tax shift would reward businesses that downsize their unproductive kilowatt-hours instead of their workforces. And individuals would profit by choosing energy-misers when buying new light bulbs, appliances, and homes—as many are now discovering.

Better energy efficiency doesn't necessarily mean investing in new technologies. It often simply means adopting solutions already at hand: 65 percent of American households have at least one ceiling fan; almost a quarter have three or more fans. Resorting to air-conditioning only when fans alone can't handle the job can yield bigger energy savings than investing in a new cooling system. Other simple measures—such as kicking off your shoes, sipping a cool drink, or growing shade trees around the house—are all energy-efficient ways of cooling down. Because an office worker feels about 5°F (3°C) warmer in a coat and tie than in a short-sleeve shirt, simply allowing employees to dress casually can save an office roughly three hundred dollars per employee in cooling and electrical equipment costs and perhaps ten dollars per employee in annual air-conditioning bills.

What's ironic—or perhaps tragic—about the world's environmental undoing is that so little of it does anyone any good. So much of the climate-warming pollution blown out of smokestacks ultimately serves only to heat or cool air that leaks through building windows and walls. So many natural gas turbines serve only to create unwanted heat, from light bulbs or friction in poorly built appliance motors. So many atomic reactions provide heat that no one ever feels—studies show that in most American households, no one bothers to adjust the thermostat when the home is empty or when everyone is asleep.

The flip side of this irony is that doing the right thing—using energy efficiently the way a ceiling fan does—is no sacrifice; on the contrary, it's financially and emotionally rewarding. With a ceiling fan spinning overhead, there's no need to feel uncomfortable about making ourselves comfortable.

⟦ *The Clothesline* ⟧

SUSAN WARNER LIVES IN THE MIDDLE of a rain forest—
in Juneau, Alaska—but she loves hanging clothes up to
dry. "I like seeing laundry," the working mother ex-
plains. "Last weekend, our neighbor had pretty colored
sheets hanging in the wind, and I really appreciated it.
Where my parents live now in California, they're not
even allowed to use clotheslines."

It rains every other day in Juneau, and hypother-
mia-inducing drizzle seems to threaten year-round, yet
Sue and husband Ken have no dryer in the laundry
room of their 1913 home in Juneau's downtown his-
toric district. Sue relies mostly on foldable wooden racks
in her basement. "Why would I want a dryer?" she asks.
"I mean, clothes dry by themselves!"

In its day, more than a century ago, the clothesline
was cutting-edge technology. Today it is sometimes
illegal, at least outdoors, but it remains a simple, silent,
and completely nonpolluting alternative to the dryer,

one of the domestic world's biggest producers of climate-altering carbon.

Clotheslines do require more time and effort than dryers, but if Susan can line-dry her clothes in North America's rainiest city, anyone can. Clotheslines are simple, silent, and completely nonpolluting. They take few materials to manufacture and require no electricity or fuel to operate. A new one costs about ten dollars and saves hundreds. It installs in minutes. Line-dried clothes smell fresh and have no static, and people who air-dry their laundry outside get in touch with the weather, which flowers are in bloom, and who their neighbors are.

Moreover, clotheslines are an elegant illustration of how renewable energy in all forms can go a long way toward reducing humanity's carbon output. By letting the sun and wind do for free what dryers need electricity or gas for, clotheslines also save money. Diehard users avoid the expense of a new dryer, but even dryer owners save money by hanging clothes on the line whenever time and weather permit. In a typical home, the clothes dryer uses much less electricity than central air-conditioning or a refrigerator but more than any other appliance. Feeding the dryer electricity will cost nearly $100 a year, $1,400 over its lifetime. Because clothes last longer when they're spared a tumble dryer's heat and wear and tear, clotheslines also protect the $1,400 that the average American household invests in new clothing each year. Just look in any dryer's lint trap to see the damage done as clothes shake and bake.

Sadly, clotheslines have fallen out of fashion. The automatic dryer, first manufactured in 1939, started becoming popular in the postwar appliance frenzy of the 1950s. In 1960, less than a fifth of American households, and only an eighth of Canadian households, had automatic dryers. Today three-fourths of both nations' households have dryers; only 15 percent of U.S. households even occasionally line-dry their clothing. Many apartment buildings and homeowners' associations have gone so far as to ban clotheslines entirely.

But it takes only a slight shift in viewpoint to see clotheslines—and the energy that makes them work—in a different light. Although solar, wind, geothermal, and biomass power officially contribute 4 percent to current global energy supplies, we already use these renewable energy sources—the sun, above all—in unacknowledged ways. Solar designer-philosopher Steve Baer has dubbed this "the clothesline paradox": dry your laundry in an electric dryer, and the electricity you use is counted in conventional energy statistics, but dry your clothes on a clothesline instead, and the solar and wind energy you harness is never measured. The sun, of course, also heats our entire world from about −400°F (−240°C) to livable temperatures, but we only count as "energy use" the amount required to heat or cool the insides of our buildings the last few degrees to room temperature.

The decline and fall of the clothesline have come at a price to the Earth's temperature. A typical North American family of four does about six loads of laundry a week and devotes about 5 percent of its annual electricity use to the dryer. With the mix of fuels burned to generate U.S. electricity, the average household dryer puts almost a ton of climate-damaging carbon dioxide into the atmosphere per year. The heating coils in most dryers (only 20 percent of American dryers heat with gas) require about three kilowatt-hours of electricity per load, enough to read by the light of a sixty-watt bulb for two days or work on a laptop computer for a week.

Like many appliances, new dryers are more efficient than old ones. Moisture sensors in today's dryer drums can save about 15 percent of the energy used when relying on a dryer's timer. On the horizon is the microwave clothes dryer, which offers a potential 28 to 40 percent savings. But none of these technologies can match the 100 percent savings of the simple clothesline.

The Clothesline

By drawing on the wind and sun, the clothesline avoids all the environmental impacts of electricity and natural gas. The clothesline is one of an array of technologies—from the ancient to the avant-garde—that fight global warming, acid rain, nuclear waste, and a host of other ills. These pervasive energy-related problems have twin solutions: using energy more efficiently (see "The Ceiling Fan") and shifting as quickly as possible to renewable energy sources.

Fortunately, renewable energy is superabundant, and the cost of tapping into it is falling rapidly. In an hour and fifteen minutes, the Earth receives as much energy in the form of sunlight as humans officially use in a year. If American rooftops were covered with solar shingles, they could supply half to three-quarters of the country's present energy needs; winds in the United States are capable of supplying roughly one and a half times all the electricity used nationwide. Capturing a tiny fraction of these abundant resources would go a long way toward meeting the world's energy demands.

The clothesline is only the most obvious way to tap into the renewable energy all around us. Considering the energy used to heat water, washing a load of clothes in warm water actually uses about twice as much energy as heating the load in a dryer. (Water heating accounts for nearly 20 percent of home energy use in the United States.) Rooftop solar water heaters use the sun to heat and natural convection to pump water into a home water tank. It can take several years to recoup the initial costs of these simple but pricey systems, depending on energy prices and how much sun smiles on your home. China has installed roughly 30 million solar hot water heaters.

Homes and businesses can be (and are) heated, cooled, lit, and powered by solar energy in its various forms. "Passive solar" design, such as well-placed windows and overhangs that let in warm light from the low-hanging winter sun but not from the high summer sun, can minimize or eliminate the need for heating and air-conditioning. Even in the cloudy Pacific Northwest, passive solar design can supply 65 percent of a home's space heating. As an ad for Velux windows says of sunlight, "It traveled millions of miles to get here. The least you can do is let it in."

Half a million homes worldwide generate their own solar power with photovoltaic (PV) cells. PVs are wafer-thin semiconductors that turn light into electricity; they are probably most familiar as the power source for many hand-held calculators. Solar cells provide a minuscule share of the world's electricity, but their sales have boomed since 1990. The number of solar panels sold in the United States increased more than tenfold between 1996 and 2005, when enough solar panels were sold in the United States to produce 140 megawatts, or the power of a small power plant.

Production costs are dropping rapidly as sales multiply, though PV-generated power still costs too much to compete except in remote locations. Much like related computer chip technology, PV technology is advancing swiftly, and major corporations like BP and Shell are making multimillion-dollar investments. A recent California law mandates the addition of one million solar roofs by 2018, and any developer building more than fifty new homes must have a solar panel option by 2011. Still, it's likely that, as clothes dryers and energy-inefficient buildings replace clotheslines and passive solar practices in the developing world, solar energy's real share of world energy use is declining.

Circulation in the atmosphere is driven by differences in the amount of solar energy reaching different parts of the Earth. Humans have harnessed the resulting energy in windmills, sails, and other technologies for millennia. As in passive solar design, buildings can be designed (and operated) to take advantage of the prevailing air movements. Opening the windows on opposite sides of a house harnesses wind energy for good cross-ventilation. A "thermal chimney"—which can be created simply by opening first-floor windows and a window at the top of the stairs to the second floor—draws breezes through the house because warm air rises and is replaced by cooler air below.

A more sophisticated means of capturing wind energy, wind turbines convert wind into electricity. Wind power provides less than 1 percent of world electricity, but capacity is expanding at a rate of 25 percent per year, making wind the world's fastest-growing energy source. The cost of wind-generated electricity in the United States has dropped from 25 cents per kilowatt-hour in 1984 to less than 5 cents per kilowatt-hour today, making it competitive with coal and cheaper than nuclear power. Wind now creates 2 percent of the United States' electricity, accounting for 11,000 megawatts, and it is expected to reach 49,000 megawatts by 2015. In some regions of Europe, wind power already supplies 5 to 10 percent of electricity.

Modern wind turbines are much quieter than their predecessors; most people cannot hear them three hundred yards away. Some nature lovers fear that wind farms will endanger bird populations, but studies in Europe have concluded that well-designed and well-sited wind farms pose little risk to birds. A study for the Danish Ministry of the Environment found that power lines, including those leading to wind farms, endanger birds much more than do wind turbines themselves. And climate change itself is a major threat to our feathered friends.

Realizing the promise of renewables will take more than concerned individuals using clotheslines or rooftop solar panels. Building market volumes sufficient to bring prices down will require large-scale investments. In 1997 the U.S. Department of Energy launched a "million roofs" initiative aimed at installing solar systems on a million U.S. buildings, but the program fell several hundred thousand roofs short for lack of funding. The U.S million roofs initiative became the Solar America Initiative in 2006, allocating $168 million to R&D, but it hardly compares to California's Million Solar Roofs initiative, which provides $3.2 billion in rebates for solar roof installation.

Shifting to renewable energy sources and reducing the amount of energy we waste are the keys to reducing the bloated impact of industrial nations on the atmosphere. To stabilize the world's climate, industrial nations will also need to help provide alternatives to fossil fuels in the developing world. Otherwise, the two billion people in the world without electricity, and the many who have a little but want more, will turn to the world's vast supplies of heavily polluting coal to meet their energy needs.

While European nations have begun taxing fossil fuels to discourage their combustion, U.S. and Canadian government policies make these fuels artificially cheap, discouraging investment in renewable alternatives. The U.S. tax code provides $31.6 billion in subsidies for the oil and gas industry. Canada's oil and gas producers also receive more than a billion dollars a year.

In short, if investors and energy users had to pay (through taxes or other mechanisms, such as a cap and trade program) for all the pollution, health problems, and climate change caused by fossil fuels, renewables would quickly take over the world energy market. Clotheslines would spring up in North American back-yards faster than dandelions, and energy-efficient front-loading washing machines—which use less hot water than top-loading machines and make drying easier with their faster spin cycles—would quickly turn today's top-loaders into an icon of wasteful decades past.

Individuals usually have lacked the power to choose renewable energy (except with actions like drying clothes in the sun), but that may soon change. More than six hundred regulated utilities in more than thirty states now offer "green" pricing programs, and green tags and renewable energy certificates can be purchased from many organizations around the country. Some states offer tax incentives for installing renewable-energy systems.

Running through the tangle of policy, economics, and technology that surrounds renewable energy, the simple clothesline promises that we can meet our needs without overwhelming the Earth. In 1997, when student activists at Vermont's Middlebury College wanted to protest nuclear energy, they organized students across New England to hang their sheets out on clotheslines as a symbolic protest. Their simple message: a sustainable energy economy can begin in our own backyards.

⟦ *The Real Tomato* ⟧

FOR MUCH OF THE YEAR, a hundred-plus farmers from across Washington State make weekly pilgrimages to Seattle, bringing the tastes of the countryside to small neighborhood farmers' markets scattered around the city. Billy Allstot brings strawberries, peppers, and eggplants from the Okanogan Valley. Dennis Schultz brings kiwis from his Green Water Farm on the Olympic Peninsula. And if it's Thursday, you'll find Richard Ness in the Lake City neighborhood overseeing tables of fresh-picked gems with names like Kellogg's Breakfast, Cherokee Purple, Yellow Brandywine, and White Queen.

Shoppers stand two and three deep, paying a pre-mium price. "They want it fresh," says Ness, who farms in Ellensburg, in the Kittitas Valley, just east of the Cascade Mountains. "They're demanding people."

Vine-ripened, truly flavorful tomatoes like Ness's are a staple of farmers' markets, a growing institution with more than four thousand franchises across the nation. Ness's tomatoes are lessons in the merits of a fresh fruit or vegetable, alive with tangy and sometimes exotic flavor, a voyage of culinary discovery as old as the Aztecs.

They also show how far the tomato has come. Too far, if you're considering the thing most often called a tomato these days.

It started as a wild fruit in the Andes of western South America, then was a farmed fruit among the Aztecs of Central America. There it fell into the hands and mouths of Spanish conquistadors, priests, and functionaries, who introduced it to the Philippines, the Caribbean, and Europe. Colonists brought it back across the Atlantic to North America, where eventually food packers found a way to squeeze billions of them into narrow-necked bottles of ketchup that lurk in seven out of nine refrigerators.

The tomato—botanically a fruit but legally a vegetable after an 1893 U.S. Supreme Court decision—is ubiquitous and hugely popular, the second most common fresh vegetable after lettuce. It is also infamous, reduced over the years from a juicy grenade of flavor to the mealy, bland, thick-skinned hardball that some shoppers now think of as the norm.

"People have gotten used to a hard tomato," says Ness, who grows a dozen varieties of old-line heirloom tomatoes. "If they come by a soft one, they think it's 'spoiled.'"

Today's supermarket-issue tomato is a road warrior, picked apple-hard and "mature green," then ethylene gassed to a pale-red illusion of ripeness. It makes up the bulk of the fresh tomato crop, tolerating rough handling, long bouts of storage and display, and lots of travel. Tomatoes can grow in all fifty states, but just two—California and Florida—account for two-thirds of the fresh tomatoes grown in the country. Along with the rest of our nation's fresh vegetables, they travel 1,500 to 2,500 miles to market, according to several studies.

As recently as the 1950s, the fruits and vegetables eaten in most major cities were grown on nearby farms, a likely reason New Jersey, lying between the cities of New York and Philadelphia, came to be called "the Garden State." But refrigerated transport, interstates, and advances in storage quickly took the show on the road. By 1996, more than 90 percent of fresh produce was moving by truck, according to research by David and Marcia Pimentel, authors of *Food, Energy, and Society*. And the distance food travels is only growing longer as global trade and cheap oil make it easier to send produce around the planet. Almost 900 billion tons of food were shipped worldwide in 2002, a fourfold increase from

1961. More than one-fourth of Americans' fresh fruits were imported in 2001, more than double the amount in 1985. Imports also account for a third of America's fruit juices, more than half its asparagus—and more than a third of its tomatoes.

So even in the peak of summer, when tomatoes are ripening in gardens around the country, American supermarkets will sell mass-produced hothouse tomatoes from Canada and Roma tomatoes from Mexico. The result: tens of thousands of tons of carbon dioxide emissions, often when nearby food choices can be grown, processed, and shipped with much less energy. As things are, the hundreds of gallons of oil used to feed each American citizen every year produce more than a ton of carbon dioxide.

It used to be that agriculture was largely solar powered: crops grew in the sun, and humans and animals, powered by those very crops, harvested them. Now agriculture is in many ways a study in the flow of fossil fuels. Gas, diesel, and coal are factors in almost every step of production, creating inorganic fertilizers and synthetic pesticides, pumping water for irrigation, driving complex machinery and powerful tractors. By the Pimentels' account, the U.S. food system uses nearly one-fifth of the nation's energy supply.

More than most other industries, agriculture arouses our sense that things are askew in our environment. Perhaps it is because we expect so much from farms. They are a last refuge for the eye in a world of highways, strip malls, and cul-de-sacs, and they evoke nostalgia about country living and traditional values, like physical labor and working in sync with the seasons. So it's disappointing to find that agriculture is the leading source of water pollution and the biggest water consumer in North America, as well as the main force behind soil erosion and the loss of wetlands and grasslands.

But as Americans learn more about agriculture's impact, more and more consumers are stepping outside of the mainstream food system with choices aimed at healthier bodies, cleaner landscapes, and a smaller carbon footprint. They're seeking out farmers' markets, buying food directly from local farmers with more sustainable practices, and sometimes raising food in their home gardens. They're eating more organic food. Or they're cutting back on burgers and other meat in favor of equally tasty meatless options—substituting the beefsteak (tomato) for beef and steak.

A diet that's relatively low in animal protein is better for the environment. Fruits and vegetables require two calories of energy inputs to produce one calorie of output. Animal proteins, on the other hand, take any-where from twenty to eighty calories of energy to produce one calorie.

In the United States, people eat more meat and poul-try (two hundred pounds a year on average) than in any other nation, consuming vast amounts of energy in the process. Livestock production consumes almost half the energy used in American agriculture; in Canada, farm animals eat over three times more grain than humans do. About seven pounds of grain are needed to produce a pound of boneless, trimmed pork; about three pounds for each pound of chicken; and, depending on how much time cattle spend grazing before entering a feedlot, about five pounds for a pound of beef.

In almost every category of concern associated with agriculture—water and energy consumption, erosion, overgrazing, pollution, even methane emissions—grains and vegetables are hands-down winners over livestock. A pound of beef produced in the United States sends about a half-pound of methane into the atmosphere— the greenhouse equivalent of burning half a gallon of gasoline. That's six times more than what a pound of American-grown rice generates. Globally, livestock and manure produce about three times more methane than rice paddies.

Jamais Cascio, futurist and co-founder of the environmental blog WorldChanging.com, has calculated the carbon footprint of the cheeseburger and concluded that "the greenhouse gas emissions arising every year from the production and consumption of cheeseburgers are roughly the amount emitted by 6.5 million to 19.6 million SUVs." To put that in perspective, consider that that there are about 16 million SUVs on the road in the United States.

The problems arising from animal agriculture are vexing enough with just one in four people worldwide eating a meat-centered diet. There's no way the world can support 6 billion—much less a future population of 8 to 12 billion—heavy meat eaters. For everyone in the world today to eat an American-style diet, farmers would have to grow nearly three times as much grain as they do now. Steer number 534, an Angus calf that author Michael Pollan followed from pasture to feedlot, indirectly consumed nearly a barrel of oil (that's forty-two gallons) to reach slaughter weight.

The staggering waste of crops required by the North American diet does not mean that world hunger is caused by people eating cheeseburgers. Most of the world's 840 million malnourished people simply lack the money and land to buy or grow enough food. Eating lower on the food chain won't do much to solve the problem of global hunger; only a frontal attack on the root causes of poverty can do that. Yet as the number of mouths to feed keeps growing, land now used to grow feed crops could be needed to fight hunger in the future.

Asian-style diets make the most of increasingly scarce cropland: it takes about an acre of pasture and cropland to support the average Chinese person's diet, while it takes about four acres, which would cover nearly four football fields, to support the average American.

Eating organic can also go a long way to reduce the environmental impact of your menu. Fossil fuel–based synthetic fertilizers and pesticides account for more than one-third of the energy used on U.S. farms. Agronomists comparing organic and conventional farming have also found that organic farms leave soils healthier.

But organic food can fall short when food miles start entering the equation. A recent study by student researchers at the University of Alberta compared organic and conventionally grown produce and found that many organic products traveled farther to reach Edmonton stores, with mangoes coming from as far away as Peru. Transporting organic produce into a city the size of Edmonton generated as much if not more carbon dioxide than conventional produce, they said.

One might make a case that the benefits of organic food outweigh such drawbacks; for example, organic food grown with on-site manure (one of the most energy-efficient ways of farming organically) will use one-third less fossil fuel on the farm than does conventionally grown food. But some foods don't add up so well.

Bottled water is a notorious carbon culprit. Every day, Americans go through 40 million bottles of water. The bottles are usually made from petroleum-based plastic, and the vaunted water often comes from a regular old public drinking supply. The bottles must be shipped, often over large distances.

Using a ratio of food miles to calories, bottled water is an enormous waste. It's a waste of money, too. New York City officials recently calculated that eight glasses of city tap water a day costs forty-nine cents a year. That same amount in bottled water costs about $1,400 a year.

If you are among those who regularly think of beer as an alternative to water, think again. A study of wine, beer, and spirits in Britain found that the resources required to get both your beer and you to the pub—including crops, production, packaging, refrigeration, and transport—account for almost 1.5 percent of the United Kingdom's greenhouse-gas emissions. Just moving that nation's supply of alcohol produces the equivalent of nearly a quarter-million tons of CO_2.

Even a seemingly innocent one-pound bag of lettuce can be a fossil-fuel glutton, consuming 4,600 calories to grow, process, and ship an item that is mostly water and contains a scant eighty calories of food energy. Joan Gussow, a Columbia University nutritionist, calls this "burning lots of petroleum to ship cold water around."

Annika Carlsson-Kanyama, a Swedish researcher who specializes in the environmental impacts of consumption and production, looked at the energy involved in producing 150 different food items and found that individual choices can play a huge role in a meal's carbon count. A dinner of beef, rice, greenhouse tomatoes, and wine used three times as much energy per serving as one of chicken, potatoes, carrots, and tap water. "Up to a third of the total energy inputs is related to snacks, sweets, and drinks, items with little nutritional value," she concluded.

In the past few years, more and more people have sought to get around whole sectors of the food system by going back to the farm. Restaurants are serving local and seasonal fare, while consumers are buying food direct from farms through community-supported agriculture programs and by visiting farmers' markets. Launched in

1996, the Chefs Collaborative now has more than a thousand members promoting sustainable cuisine, often through local and seasonal foods. CSAs, also known as subscription farming, generally have customers pay farmers for a yearly share of their production and receive fruits and vegetables as they become available. A national database at the Robyn Van En Center for CSA Resources in Chambersburg, Pennsylvania, lists some 1,200 operations.

Shifting toward a diet composed of dishes where meat is the flavoring, not the substance, also can cut the climate impact of our food down to size. Replace a serving of grain-fed chicken with a grain product like rice or pasta, and you've cut in half your food's impact. You'll do even better—for the environment and for your health—if you substitute grains or vegetables for a serving of red meat. Grains, fruits, vegetables, and beans are almost always lower in fat (especially artery-clogging saturated fat) than meats.

The three most popular "ethnic" foods in North America—Italian, Mexican, and Chinese—are, generally speaking, based on grains (think pasta, tortillas, and rice). At least in their unadulterated forms, they incorporate less meat than the standard American or Canadian diet. For years, health experts have advised North

Americans to eat like peasants: *paisanos* of southern Italy or Mexican *campesinas* eat much less meat than restaurant-goers in America.

Yet you needn't have exotic tastes or access to ethnic restaurants to enjoy plant-based foods. Some of the most familiar American foods, like chicken noodle soup, baked potatoes, or peanut butter and jelly, are skimpy on animal products and environmental impact. Even macaroni and cheese (which is practically Canada's national food) fits the bill. The key is to restructure your diet, one meal at a time: try putting rice, pasta, bread, or vegetables at the center of the dish and add meat only for flavoring. Try going meatless a couple of days a week.

Or take a cue from the "locavores"—those who restrict themselves to foods produced within a hundred-mile radius of their home—as well as others less strictly devoted to eating within their local "foodshed." The hundred-mile movement has been the subject of several books, some of which have a hair-shirt air of sacrifice and struggle that makes for good reading and intimidation in equal measures. In Plenty, Vancouver, B.C., journalists Alisa Smith and James MacKinnon tell of going months without bread, then finding wheat laced with mice droppings. The last locavore act of their first year involved driving across Vancouver Island and rowing out to the

Pacific Ocean for salt water to boil down for salt. It's a pleasant enough outing, but with its own unique carbon price tag.

In general, though, the local diet has a lot going for it—supporting small family farms, living off the barcode, eating with the seasons, helping the local economy, appreciating where you live through what you eat. Eating local also has a good chance of producing fewer emissions. Richard Pirog of Iowa State University's Leopold Center for Sustainable Agriculture calculates that the continent-spanning food distribution system uses four to seventeen times the fossil fuel, and emits five to seventeen times the total carbon dioxide emissions of a local system.

The Locavores, a San Francisco group, has a useful set of guidelines for weighing what to buy: If you can't buy food that's locally produced, buy organic. If not organic, then produce from a family farm. If not a family farm, choose a local business or a "terroir" product famous for the region it's grown in, like cheese from Brie, France. And by all means, hit the farmers' market and build meals around what you find—fresh basil, a head of cauliflower, or a bag of Roma-style Patrona tomatoes.

Handle them with care; they're meant for eating, not traveling.

⟦ *The Library Book* ⟧

LOOK OUT OF ANY WINDOW at the public library in Renton, Washington, and you'll see at least four lanes of traffic racing through the center of this industrial suburb south of Seattle. But look down and you may see muscular flashes of red and green, the mating dance of sockeye salmon spawning in shallow water. Renton's library straddles the Cedar River—home to Washington's largest sockeye run. It's not exactly an idyllic setting, with 150,000 vehicles rumbling by on Interstate 405 each day. But, unlike perhaps any other library, it's a terrific place for watching salmon.

Libraries are also great places for saving salmon—and polar bears, and other endangered species, though they're not built with that purpose in mind. By sharing books, periodicals, and other materials with an entire community, a library makes thousands of personal copies unnecessary. By reducing the demand for paper, libraries help save forests from logging (so they can work their wonders of carbon storage), salmon streams from logging-road erosion and pulp mill effluent, and greenhouse-gas-belching electric grids from the power load of pulp and paper mills. The average North American library lends out a hundred thousand books a year but buys fewer than five thousand, saving nearly fifty tons of paper. In the process, it avoids the huge amounts of greenhouse-gas emissions, energy consumption, and resource waste associated with producing all that paper. A typical U.S. library prevents 250 tons of greenhouse-gas emissions each year, just from the paper it doesn't consume.

The essential wonder of libraries is that they reduce the need for newly manufactured goods. The world's biggest climate polluter is not the automobile. It's the feeding end of the global industrial economy: the extraction and processing of wood and paper, metals and other minerals, oil and petrochemicals, and other natural resources; the manufacturing of these commodities into products; and the transporting of them to consumers. In the United States, the manufacturing sector alone—not counting resource extraction or freight hauling—puts out a quarter of all greenhouse gases. That's more climate damage than even automobiles cause.

The simplest and most potent antidote to this juggernaut of industrial production is for consumers to share the final goods. That's the practice libraries institu-tionalize. Books are wonders in themselves, of course: if more people could and would read, the world would undoubtedly be a better place. But books also speak vol-umes, you might say, about the climate impact of making new things. Manufacturing uses vast amounts of natural resources and energy, and creates a huge carbon footprint in the process. Quite often, used things will do just fine.

And the substance that the printed word arrives on—paper—carries a high climate price tag. Packaging, advertising, office paper, and various forms of print publishing have tripled over the past three decades and are expected to grow again by half before 2010. Oddly, this growth is in part because allegedly "paperless" com-puters are so good at printing en masse. That little "print" button can start more chainsaws felling the world's forests and send a witches' brew of chemical pollutants spewing into its rivers and bays.

Better to make trees a global-warming solution, not part of the problem. Trees are marvelous warehouses of carbon. Oregon State University researchers say that ecosystems in their state alone stored about 30 million tons of carbon dioxide per year between 1996 and 2000. That's almost enough to offset the state's total annual emissions of CO_2.

A century of logging in Pacific Northwest forests released close to 2 billion tons of carbon, according to Mark Harmon, an OSU forest ecologist. At current rates of emissions, that's roughly equivalent to a year's worth of greenhouse gases from all 300 million Americans. If today's harvesters waited longer between harvests, they could as much as double the carbon-storage of a forest and still produce timber products, according to a study by the Pacific Forest Trust.

Despite increased paper recycling, pulp and paper mills digest about 40 percent of the global timber harvest. A relatively small number of consumers in wealthy nations use most of the world's paper: the United States alone, with less than 5 percent of world population, consumes one-third of the world's paper production. Each American goes through roughly two pounds of paper a day, while the U.S. pulp and paper industry is the nation's second-largest industrial consumer of energy.

All of this ends up putting out a lot of carbon. Paper and paperboard mills produced the greenhouse-gas equivalent of more than 100 million metric tons in 2002—and that's not counting newsprint, according to the Energy Information Administration. Only petroleum refineries and iron and steel mills produced more.

Fortunately, books and other paper products can be enjoyed at a fraction of their current climate impact if they are given second chances at life. We're not talking about recycling, either. Recycling is great, but it doesn't deserve its status as poster child for ecological living. In the familiar mantra "reduce, reuse, recycle," the imperatives are listed in priority order: recycling is only a bronze medalist in environmental protection.

To produce a book of 100 percent recycled paper, a paper mill uses about 60 percent of the energy and generates half the solid waste, one-third the greenhouse gases, and 95 percent of·the effluent of a mill producing the average U.S. book. To produce "100 percent reused" library books, paper mills (and printing presses) use zero energy and generate zero pollution per new reader, since reuse bypasses the production stage altogether.

On average, Americans each buy some eight books a year and borrow about seven books and other items from a library. (Canadians each buy an estimated three books and borrow almost five items.) Our library readings come at a fraction of the economic and ecological cost of our bookstore purchases. A U.S. library book is on average borrowed 2.4 times a year; a Canadian book, 3.4 times. If one of these books lasts even four years, at least ten people will enjoy it during its shelf life, instead of the one or two who might read the same book pur-chased in a store. In other words, library patrons enjoy reading at one-fifth or one-tenth the impact of book-store customers.

To be sure, books are responsible for a small share of paper consumption; packaging, magazines, newspapers, catalogs, and office paper all use bigger portions of the world's timber supply. But libraries lend out much more than books. The repeated use of any library materials—periodicals, audio and video materials, even computer terminals, a growing service—makes similar resource savings possible.

Whatever materials they lend, libraries save money by using resources efficiently. Even taking into account the twenty dollars in taxes that the average American pays to support public libraries, he or she saves at least twice that a year by borrowing half a dozen or so free books from a library instead of buying them. They yield a great return on their investment. The King County Library System in Washington (home to the salmon-rich Renton library) returns five dollars in library benefits for each tax dollar; Phoenix returns ten dollars.

All libraries—private, academic, or public—serve as important repositories of knowledge and centers of learning, yet the public library undoubtedly brings the greatest benefits: a book borrowed from a public library is most likely to take the place of a book purchased from a store. Even more, the public library is the most democratic of institutions: free and open to all on an equal basis, dedicated to maintaining an informed and literate citizenry. Public libraries in the United States host five times as many visitors as all major professional and college sporting events combined. Libraries also foster a sense of community by bringing together people of all backgrounds and ages into a welcoming public space, one of North America's most endangered human habitats.

Libraries are just one of many forms of institutionalized sharing or reuse: renting, buying secondhand, and repairing instead of throwing away are all familiar ways people get the most out of scarce goods. There's no reason the library concept can't be expanded to include a whole variety of useful items. More than twenty U.S. cities have tool libraries where local residents can borrow hedge trimmers, ladders, table saws, and more. The most popular form of reuse currently may be movie rental: video stores outnumber public libraries, and consumers rent three times as many DVDs as they buy.

Checking out a video uses fewer resources than buying one, but it still carries an ecological cost: a trip to the video store may only replace a trip to the movie theater, while the average video renter's three-mile drive to reach a favorite store (scary how much industry marketers know about their customers, isn't it?) just about cancels out the petroleum saved in not manufacturing a DVD. But the popularity of video rentals shows that, if the price and infrastructure are right, North Americans have no problems with reusing stuff. And online services like Netflix subtract driving from video rental's carbon footprint.

EBay has also done wonders for the reuse way of life, posting more than 6 million listings a day. This global, digital garage sale keeps millions of otherwise worthless used consumer goods—think of them as little chunks of embodied greenhouse gases—out of landfills. It prevents the manufacture of new replacements when the world already has enough. Just so, the classified ad Web site Craigslist turns tens of millions of one-way consumption stories into closed-loop stories of reuse— a for-profit form of sharing. In 2007, the Web site posted 14 million classified ads—drawing 22 million unique visitors—every month. It saves some paper by displacing classified newspaper ads, but it also prevents the manufacture (and climatic repercussions) of new goods.

Used merchandise stores are a thriving business, too, with low capital costs, low-cost inventory, and

Small Wonder: The Reused Envelope

Those old-fashioned interdepartmental envelopes that close with a string are the cutting edge of Earth-friendly packaging. Covered with spaces for writing successive addresses, they are designed to be reused thirty times or more. They put modern recycling—and the shipping industry—to shame.

Overnight and express shippers in the United States deliver more than a billion envelopes and boxes annually, most of them trashed after one use. Until fairly recently, if you tried to reuse one of FedEx's signature white cardboard envelopes, you'd be told the company forbade reuse. FedEx has improved its packaging performance, with more recycled and recyclable materials, no bleaching, and a reusable envelope to replace the old Express Letter—realizing a 12 percent reduction in net greenhouse gases from its production, according to the company. UPS also has a reusable next-day air envelope, but it only works twice.

In United States, almost all shipments arrive in disposable cardboard boxes. Despite a recycling rate of around 70 percent, containerboard is the single largest component of the nation's waste stream. What would the world look like if documents and goods traveled instead in "interdestinational" packaging, with crossed-out names tracing each package's many lives?

relatively high returns. They are growing by about 5 percent a year. Some 25,000 resale, consignment, and thrift shops now generate billions of dollars in sales. According to their trade association—yes, they have a trade association, the National Association of Resale and Thrift Shops—almost as many Americans will go to a thrift shop this year as will visit a clothing retailer or a major department store.

Once typified by unsavory pawnshops and charity stores full of barely salable merchandise, secondhand stores have become popular among middle-class shoppers who love bargains and relish fashion points scored with shabby-chic or stylish retro finds, even if they don't realize that used goods cost the Earth next to nothing. National chains have moved in to capitalize on the popularity of used clothing; for-profit and nonprofit secondhand stores now sell everything from antique furniture to used sporting goods, CDs, and computer software. Savers Inc., which operates more than two hundred Savers, Value Village, and Village des Valeurs shops in the United States and Canada, also helps incubate nonprofits that collect used goods to raise money for their services. Nearly half the goods are shipped to developing nations and material recyclers.

Unfortunately, many forms of reuse have fallen out of favor as acquisition has replaced neighborly borrowing and other forms of sharing, and as cheap appliances and semidisposable furniture have replaced durability and repair. Elementary school cafeterias featured bottles of milk as recently as the 1970s. Once-commonplace refillable soda bottles are a nostalgic relic to Americans, though alive and well in other nations. In Canada, over 97 percent of beer bottles are returned for refilling; in Denmark, 99 percent of all soda and beer bottles are refilled. Even including washing, the use of refillables saves 90 percent or more of the materials and energy—and climate damage—required to manufacture new bottles.

Reuse—institutionalized sharing—does not get enough attention as an environmental strategy, but it can help us quickly find our way out of the ecological pinch we're in. While industry and government spend millions on recycling campaigns, refillable bottles fight pollution and waste without fanfare and more effectively. Even as cutting-edge clothing manufacturers advertise their organic cotton and recycled fleece, unassuming thrift stores keep on selling the most ecologically friendly clothing of all. And while others fight noisily over who needs to do what to keep endangered species from disappearing, libraries and their kin go quietly about their business of saving rivers, forests, and our climate—one book, magazine, compact disc, and hedge trimmer at a time.

⟦ *The Microchip* ⟧

THE BUSINESS END OF A HUMAN nerve cell, a fundamental unit of our intelligence, is about one micron thick. That's one-millionth of a meter, or one-hundredth of a human hair's breadth.

The circuit of a computer microprocessor is even smaller. A recent Intel chip is so small that thirty thousand transistors—which switch the zeroes and ones that are the fundamental units of the digital world—can fit on the head of a pin. It can perform hundreds of millions of calculations in a second.

Thus far, the wonders in this book have been relatively simple devices. A kid can ride a bike, a condom fits in your wallet or purse, and a card will get you a library book. But at the risk of gumming up such elegant low-tech works, let's get complicated and consider the microprocessor, or (to keep the language simple) the chip, which Intel calls "the most complex mass-produced product ever."

A chip starts simply enough as plain silicon—sand, basically. Other metals and introduced impurities alter its conducting and insulating properties. More than 250 steps are involved in its construction, using heat, gas, chemicals, and ultraviolet light to produce a three-dimensional, multilayered package in which the space between some circuits can be just five atoms thick. Of all the inventions in history, it comes closest to rivaling the human nerve cell. And it has great potential to tackle the complicated challenge of fixing a warming atmosphere.

Like the human brain, the chip can take on a slew of complex tasks. Most are hidden in plain sight. Sure, you know there are chips working in your computer and your printer, as well as in your TV, car, camera, home phone, and cell phone. They're also in the fridge, oven, and microwave. For that matter, they're in your kids' toys, your smoke detector, that obnoxious musical birthday card, a slew of medical equipment, and your watch—even an ostensibly "analog" watch with sweeping hands and an audible ticking sound. There may be one under your pet's skin, to help identify her if she gets lost. "Intel Inside" indeed.

Like pine-tree air fresheners and butterfly tattoos, these things are everywhere. Each year, the semiconductor industry makes about 100 million transistors for every man, woman, and child on Earth. By 2010, the number should be up to 1 billion.

It's a revolutionary invention on a lot of fronts. So many technologies have transformed things in concrete, physical ways. The wheel gets you off your feet, the condom is a personal cofferdam, and the clothesline increases your shirt's surface area and raises its temperature, assisting evaporation. But like books and broadcasting, chips work in the domain of information, moving it and processing it in whole new ways.

"They are machines that produce decisions," says Jeffrey Zygmont in *Microchip: An Idea, Its Genesis, and the Revolution It Created*. On a computer, chips facilitate calculations as nuanced and complex as those required to track the warming of the atmosphere. They shepherd the Internet's millions of computers, routers, and wires, helping scientists and policy makers and activists share data and findings around the world.

And here's where the chip really stands out as a wonder among wonders: it can make us smarter, boosting the power of the human brain and its own tiny transistors to make our world a better place.

You might wonder how that's possible, when huge avenues of the Internet are clogged by "adult entertainment," vacuous YouTube videos, and more than

100 billion junk e-mails a day. Nonetheless, connected computers are a tool so powerful that a term like "Information Superhighway"—remember that one?—fails miserably as a metaphor. A superhighway calls to mind long hours in a car watching a moving wallpaper of trees and traffic. The Internet can deliver instantly. Indeed, networked chips are being used in countless energy-saving ways that brilliantly address the over-production of planet-warming carbon.

Just look at the simple acquisition of, say, a book. Before the Internet, you might have called a library to see if a book was in, but you more likely drove over and walked among the stacks. If the book wasn't there, you might have tried another library. This could kill a few hours, burning fuel much of the time.

Now you can search a library catalog online, arrange to have a book delivered to your local branch, and receive an e-mail when it is ready to pick up. Then you can econ-omize on your time and gas by including the trip among a few other errands, or ride your bike over. And countless other acquisitions don't involve driving at all: if you want to buy an album, you can purchase it from iTunes instead of at the mall.

It adds up to a perfect marriage of convenience and energy savings. Joseph Romm, executive director of the

Center for Energy and Climate Solutions and a head of the Energy Department's efficiency and renewable energy program during the Clinton administration, calculated that the energy costs per book sold are sixteen times greater for a conventional bookstore than for Amazon. Shipping ten pounds of packages by overnight air—the most energy-intensive delivery mode—still uses 40 percent less fuel than driving round-trip to the mall. (It's a different story, of course, if you walk or bike to the bookstore.) Ground shipping by truck is even better, using one-tenth the energy of driving yourself.

The Organization for Economic Co-Operation and Development figures that a broader application of Internet retailing could eliminate the need for 12.5 percent of retail building space. This is the same as 1.5 billion square feet of commercial space, saving hundreds of millions of dollars in heating costs.

Businesses are also downsizing their physical plants and energy use by using off-site workers—Web-based home businesses and home-based telecommuters created and enabled by the Internet. Between 1990 and 2000, the number of people working from home—also known as "teleworkers" and "people who work in their underwear"—grew by almost one-fourth, according to the U.S. Census Bureau. That's twice the growth rate of the general labor market. According to the Telework Coalition, nearly one in five American workers telecommute at least once a month. When they do telecommute, according to a study by the libertarian Reason Foundation, they cut their number of daily trips by as much as half and reduce their driving by as much as three-fourths. In more than half the major cities studied, they outnumber transit commuters. That's a remarkable notion: almost by accident, the Internet is as powerful as an urban transit system.

AT&T helped pioneer telecommuting as a way to save costs, using shared offices and easily rearranged work spaces. In less than ten years, it avoided 110 million miles of commuting and saved about 50,000 tons of carbon dioxide and 5.1 million gallons of gasoline. In Connecticut alone, telecommuting takes nearly 60,000 cars off the road every day. Meanwhile, studies show that telecommuting improves employee retention, increases productivity, and reduces absenteeism.

Workers can even attend meetings and conferences without leaving home through Web meeting companies like WebEx and GoToMeeting. Online video services stream conference proceedings around the planet, saving money and air travel. With the help of a ten-gigabyte fiber-optic connection and a high-definition television studio, the Seattle Science Foundation can have a San Francisco brain surgeon demonstrate his one-of-a-kind technique to doctors around the world. The Bioneers annual conference on sustainable living is beamed via satellite to more than a dozen cities around North America.

For those who must drive but don't want to own a car, car-sharing companies let users go online and find the car nearest to them, searching by zip code or by zooming in on a map. In Los Angeles, that car could be a sporty number at 213 South Spring Street or a hybrid at 312 Broadway Avenue. Directions to the car include transit information. A card reader opens and locks the car door. One car-share vehicle can displace as many as fifteen other cars, using less fuel, creating less carbon, and requiring less public infrastructure. In some ways, it's a variation on the reuse concept, multiplied by orders of magnitude through the power of the chip.

A bit of magic is at work here, or what Romm calls "e-materialization." Materials use a lot of energy to make and move, as we saw in the library chapter (see "The Library Book"). But some materials can be replaced with digital information. In other cases, information can help manage materials more efficiently.

In his paper "The Internet Economy and Global Warming," Romm wrote: "The Internet has the ability to turn retail buildings into Web sites and to turn warehouses into better supply chain software, to dematerialize paper and CDs into electrons, and to turn trucks into fiber optic cables."

To be sure, we have not become the paperless society prognosticated in the early years of the desktop computer. But e-commerce has eliminated huge amounts of the paperwork in business transactions, as have Internet-based billing systems. A study by the Boston Consulting Group estimates that the demand for paper in North America will drop by roughly one-third between 2005 and 2020, chiefly because of the Internet. And if Internet use increased just 10 percent over what the authors predicted, worldwide paper demand would drop another 4 percent, or 3 million tons. Dead trees aside, the Center for Energy and Climate Solutions says the yearly energy savings of so much saved paper is like taking 2 million cars off the road and saving 10 million metric tons of carbon dioxide.

Thanks to the Internet and deteriorating market conditions, newspapers—the largest single consumers of paper—are being read less on paper and more online. Online product and pricing information helps a company like Cisco, a computer equipment maker, save

$50 million a year. Just about anyone who can key-board "google.com" or "whowhere.com" now hardly ever reaches for a phone directory or a reference like the *Encyclopedia Britannica*, whose sales have plum-meted since 1990.

There are strong indications that the Internet is dra-matically improving manufacturing productivity. That means less heated warehouse space, less shipping in general, fewer product returns, and more direct high-volume manufacturer-to-store shipments. A reduction in new buildings alone could have a significant impact on the carbon emissions from cement production, a major source of global-warming pollution that has doubled since the mid-1970s. Romm calculates that the Internet economy could save 5 percent of U.S. commercial floor space and reduce U.S. greenhouse-gas emissions by more than 1.5 percent.

Of course, no invention is perfect.

The microchip does use electricity—lots of electricity. It has become a major player in the world's energy diet, most notably in the vast Internet processing facilities known as data centers, or server farms. Some ten thou-sand data centers operate in North America alone, hum-ming along in nondescript warehouselike facilities with little or no advertising and rigid security. They range in size from 30,000 to 300,000 square feet, and a single cabinet of servers covering just six square feet can use fifteen kilowatts, or enough power for fifteen homes. As much as half a server farm's power can go to air-conditioning alone, so that all those chips can stay at cool-enough operating temperatures.

"Computers are, for the most part, toaster ovens," one industry insider told a meeting of utility officials. "The servers inside a typical data center produce tremendous amounts of heat."

One of the largest U.S. data centers is at the Sabey Corporation's Intergate facility south of Seattle. In a single bank of servers, for example, some 27,000 users might be meeting across the miles to play an interactive game. Diesel engines stand ready in the basement to provide emergency power. Entire floors are elevated to serve as massive air-conditioning ducts, with floor vents positioned to channel air into server banks.

All those hot chips and chilled rooms add up. Jonathan Koomey, a staff scientist at the Lawrence Berkeley National Laboratory, estimates that servers, cooling, and infrastructure used 1.2 percent of the electricity produced in the U.S. in 2005. That's about as much energy as was used by color televisions, and equivalent to the energy of five large thousand-megawatt power plants.

It's also twice the amount of energy used by servers just five years earlier.

The growing energy appetite of the Internet has major players like Microsoft, Yahoo, and Google willing to invest billions of dollars to build data centers in eastern Oregon and Washington, where they can take advantage of inexpensive hydropower once used to power aluminum smelters. Sabey is getting in on the act too, with plans to move nearby and use up to thirty megawatts, one-third the capacity of the public utility district of Douglas County, Washington.

Overall, though, Internet companies' use of power is offset by gains in productivity and energy. Remember, the charm of the microchip and the Internet is that they are tools of information, and by shifting our economy toward information they have moved it away from things that use energy for production and transport. Simply put, as we make and move less stuff, we save energy. In fact, Web titan Google is prepared to spend hundreds of millions of dollars on renewable energy investments in a move that could slash its energy bills, even while it prevents pollution and ramps up clean power alternatives.

John "Skip" Laitner, an economist formerly with the EPA Office of Atmospheric Programs, notes that U.S. energy consumption grew at only half the rate of the economy from 1960 through 1996. Then the Internet began to take off and energy savings improved even more. In the next five years, energy intensity dropped more than it did during the oil crisis of the late 1970s and early 1980s. Laitner and others chalk this up to the new restructured economy as it shifted from raw materials and production to high-end value-added services, including Internet-related services.

So, yes, a microchip-based economy uses energy, but it saves energy too. Our quality of life has increased dramatically "with very little increase in power," says Sabey, who must have one of the largest utility bills in the country. "It's a very small amount relative to the value gained. You can then fast forward to how the Internet is reducing the impact of global warming dramatically. It's decreasing our overall use of power while at the same time allowing our economy to expand and our lifestyles to improve."

Even more striking is how much of this energy savings has occurred as a happy by-product of businesses trying to economize and consumers hoping to save time and money via the electronic marketplace. We have barely begun to use these new tools consciously as a way to reduce our energy use. Growing numbers of us order our DVDs online, but many of us still drive to the video store. We buy books online and drive to the mall. We can avoid paper, but we unthinkingly use more of it.

The chip stands ready to lift our efficiency to new heights. A simple programmable thermostat lets you use home heating and air conditioning only when needed and automatically turn them off when you're away. A study by Rick Heede, a greenhouse-gas analyst formerly with the Rocky Mountain Institute, found that this device offers truly impressive carbon reduction for the buck, saving the average household nearly sixty dollars and half a ton of carbon dioxide each. But programmable thermostats are installed in less than one-fourth of the nation's 106 million households. Chip-regulated devices could be saving us energy not only in our heating system but also in our computers, and in the light fixtures and appliances that draw power even when switched off.

Already the chip has made us smarter, not to mention richer. Now the challenge is to find ever more ways it can serve us in the great campaign against global warming—to make us and the planet cooler.

Appendix

Everyday Superheroes

IT'S EASY TO BE INTIMIDATED by a massive problem like climate change. It's also easy to be cynical about politicians' ability to care about anything beyond the next election.

Yet we forget how much our voices—and our choices—matter. Each of us, in fact, has power beyond our wildest dreams—superpowers, one could argue. With the flick of a wrist—reaching for organic produce instead of the conventional stuff next to it at the grocery store— you can help stop fossil fuel–based pesticides from being sprayed hundreds of miles away. That's a reach any superhero would envy. Simply by putting one foot in front of the other—walking or biking to a neighborhood shop instead of driving to the megastore on the outskirts of town—you become healthier *and* can stop oil from being drilled in some place like Nigeria or the North Slope of Alaska. Each of these actions also prevents pollution from damaging an entire planet's climate.

An entire planet's climate.

Although the cool planet wonders themselves deserve praise, it's the steps we take—making smarter choices and advocating for change—that make all the difference. Egypt's pyramids may be great even if no one gazes upon them, but a clothesline or ceiling fan saves energy only if somebody uses it. A farmers' market works its wonders only when the community shops there, and when individuals buy local foods.

In many cases, the biggest obstacle to a more climate-friendly way of life is simply habit. Yet once people start doing things differently, new practices quickly become second nature—something you do without thinking about it—and the old ways, whether it's relying on bottle-toting milkmen or lead-tainted gasoline, soon fade into memory. Recycling, for instance, has become routine for many North Americans over the past twenty years. But what would the world be like if bicycle lanes were as common and well used as recycle bins are today? What would the world be like if everyone supported reuse, energy efficiency, renewable energy, and contraception? We would quickly outflank the climate-villains of wastefulness, heedless consumption, and overpopulation that are menacing our future.

Appendix

Reading this book won't make you a superhero. But information is a crucial first step toward taking actions that will make you one. So take the next step and see what you can do in your own life. The following sources can help you learn about, use, and advocate for your favorite cool-planet wonders.

The Bicycle

Try bicycling instead of driving somewhere just once a week and see if it doesn't grow on you. Contact the organizations below or visit their Web sites, which list hundreds of local groups working to promote bicycling and to make our streets safer for everyone.

Bikely
Provides user-generated content that allows the bicycling community to share bike routes around the world.
www.bikely.com

Bikehugger
The supreme bicycling blog.
www.bikehugger.com

Surface Transportation Policy Project
1100 17th St. NW, 10th Floor
Washington, DC 20036
(202) 466-2636
www.transact.org

League of American Bicyclists
1612 K St. NW, Suite 800
Washington, DC 20006
(202) 822-1333
www.bikeleague.org

Smart Growth America
1707 L St. NW, Suite 1050
Washington, DC 20036
(202) 207-3355
www.smartgrowthamerica.org

The Condom
Never have unsafe sex. And support organizations working
to ensure that everyone else can avoid it too.

Planned Parenthood Federation of America
434 West 33rd St.
New York, NY 10001
(212) 541-7800
www.plannedparenthood.org

Population Connection
1400 16th St. NW, Suite 320
Washington, DC 20036
(800) 767-1956
www.populationconnection.org

Canadian Federation for Sexual Health
1 Nicholas St., Suite 430
Ottawa, ON K1N 7B7
(613) 241-4474
www.cfsh.ca

Guttmacher Institute
1301 Connecticut Ave. N.W., Suite 700
Washington, D.C. 20036
(877) 823-0262
www.guttmacher.org

The Ceiling Fan and the Clothesline
Under this heading are organizations that provide valuable information about climate issues and energy efficiency in general.

Rocky Mountain Institute
1739 Snowmass Creek Rd.
Snowmass, CO 81654
(970) 927-3851
www.rmi.org

1Sky
An alliance for climate action.
www.1sky.org

Step It Up
Citizen-powered activism to get our leaders to take climate change seriously.
www.stepitup2007.org

U.S. Climate Action Network
1326 14th St. NW
Washington, DC 20005
(202) 609-9846
www.usclimatenetwork.org

Climate Action Network Canada
www.climateactionnetwork.ca

David Suzuki Foundation
Suite 219, 2211 W. 4th Ave.
Vancouver, BC V6K 4S2
(800) 453-1533
www.davidsuzuki.org

Climate Solutions
219 Legion Way SW, Suite 201
Olympia, WA 98501
(360) 352-1763
www.climatesolutions.org

The Real Tomato
Support organic farmers and others who are breaking away from excessive use of chemicals and energy: buy their produce. And support the political fight for better ways to grow our food.

U.S. Agricultural Marketing Service—Farmers Markets
www.ams.usda.gov/farmersmarkets

Local Harvest
220 21st Ave.
Santa Cruz, CA 95062
(831) 475-8150
www.localharvest.org

100 Mile Diet
Tips and discussion about why—and how—to eat locally.
www.100milediet.org

Slow Food International
Revitalizing food traditions and supporting a community of thoughtful eaters.
www.slowfood.com

Appendix

The Library Book
Join or form a local "Friends of the Library" group. Or contact national library advocacy groups.

Libraries for the Future
27 Union Square West, Suite 204
New York, NY 10003
(646) 336-6236
www.lff.org

American Library Association
50 East Huron
Chicago, IL 60611
(800) 545-2433
www.ala.org

Canadian Library Association
328 Frank St.
Ottawa, ON K2P 0X8
(613) 232-9625
www.cla.ca

The Microchip
See if you can use information technology to reduce your carbon footprint. Hit the "print" button sparingly, consider commuting by data cable rather than by car, or try doing some of your holiday shopping in your pajamas.

Global Environment and Technology Foundation
2900 South Quincy St., Suite 410
Arlington, VA 22206
(703) 379-2713
www.getf.org

Sources

The research for *Seven Wonders for a Cool Planet* comes from a wide variety of sources—too many to list here—as well as from research conducted by Sightline Institute over many years. Following are descriptions of the principal research sources for each of the chapters. Readers can direct further questions to Sightline, *www.sightline.org*.

Introduction

Readers can find information about the history of climate science at the website of the American Institute of Physics, "The Discovery of Global Warming," *www.aip.org/history/climate/timeline.htm*. Especially motivated readers can also consult the comprehensive bibliography, *www.aip.org/history/climate/bib.htm*. There are many other helpful resources for understanding the history of the science, but the definitive source is The Intergovernmental Panel on Climate Change, *Fourth Assessment Report*, "Working Group I Report: The Physical Science Basis," especially Chapter 1: Historical Overview of Climate

Change Science, *www.ipcc.ch*. Sources for other facts in the Introduction can be found under the chapter headings below.

The Bicycle

Sources for "The Bicycle" included dozens of publications from government agencies, such as Statistics Canada, Transport Canada, the U.S. Department of Energy, the U.S. Census Bureau, the U.S. Department of Transportation, and the Washington Department of Transportation. Sightline also consulted publications from the National Safety Council, the International Police Mountain Bike Association, the Human Factors and Ergonomics Society, the Bicycle Helmet Safety Institute, the American Automobile Manufacturers Association, Environmental Working Group, and Worldwatch Institute. In addition, Sightline consulted academic research from the public health centers at Harvard University and Johns Hopkins University, as well as peer-reviewed articles from the *Journal of the American Medical Association*. This chapter was also informed by two of Sightline's published books: *The Car and the City* by Alan Thein Durning, April 1996; and *Stuff: The Secret Lives of Everyday Things* by John C. Ryan and Alan Thein Durning, January 1997; both can be ordered through Sightline's Web site: *www.sightline.org*.

The Condom

Research for the condom chapter was based on a large number of popular, trade, and academic publications, along with findings from the following sources: the World Health Organization, the Joint United Nations Programme on HIV/AIDS, the U.S. Centers for Disease Control and Prevention, Health

Canada, the U.S. Census Bureau, Statistics Canada, the U.S. Agency for International Development, Worldwatch Institute, Alan Guttmacher Institute, and AVERT (an AIDS prevention organization). The chapter also relied on Sightline's 1997 book *Misplaced Blame: The Real Roots of Population Growth* by Alan Thein Durning and Christopher D. Crowther, available at *www.sightline.org.*

The Ceiling Fan

Key sources for "The Ceiling Fan" include Statistics Canada and the U.S. Department of Energy. In addition, Sightline relied on research from the Rocky Mountain Institute, the Lawrence Berkeley National Laboratory, Worldwatch Institute, and the U.S. Climate Action Network. Two books also informed this chapter: Ernst U. von Weizsacker, *Factor Four: Doubling Wealth, Halving Resource Use* (London: Earthscan Publications, 1998); and Sightline Institute's 1997 book *Over Our Heads: A Local Look at Global Climate* by John C. Ryan, available on Sightline's Web site at *www.sightline.org/publications/books.*

The Clothesline

The research for "The Clothesline" was derived from a few government sources, including Statistics Canada, the U.S. Census Bureau, and the U.S. Department of Energy, as well as trade groups such as the American Fiber Manufacturers Association, the Canadian Wind Energy Association, the British Wind Energy Association, and the Danish Wind Turbine Manufacturers Association. In addition, Sightline consulted research from the Rocky Mountain Institute, Dalhousie University, the Electric Power Research Institute, Worldwatch Institute, the

U.S. Climate Emergency Council, and the Renewable Energy Policy Network for the 21st Century. Finally, this chapter drew on research for Sightline's 1997 book *Stuff: The Secret Life of Everyday Things* by Alan Thein Durning, available for order via *www.sightline.org*.

The Real Tomato

Research for this chapter was drawn from the Food and Agriculture Organization of the United Nations, the Intergovernmental Panel on Climate Change, the U.S. Department of Agriculture, the U.S. Census Bureau, Statistics Canada, the U.S. Environmental Protection Agency, World Resources Institute, and Worldwatch Institute. Sightline also consulted academic research from the agriculture departments at the University of California–Davis, North Carolina State University, Iowa State University, the University of Wisconsin–Madison, and the University of Alberta. In addition, Sightline relied on research in a large number of scientific articles and popular publications. One book is especially worth mentioning: Michael Pollan, *The Omnivore's Dilemma: A Natural History of Four Meals* (New York: Penguin Press, 2006).

The Library Book

Governmental sources used in researching "The Library Book" included the U.S. Department of Education, the U.S. Department of Energy, Statistics Canada, the U.S. Census Bureau, and the Washington Department of Transportation. Others included the Canadian Library Association, the National Association of Resale and Thrift Shops, Adams Media Research, Worldwatch Institute, Co-op America, and several popular publications.

The Microchip

The microchip chapter was most influenced by Joseph Romm, especially "The Internet Economy and Global Warming," Global Environment and Technology Foundation, December 1999. Other important sources include Jonathan G. Koomey, "Estimating Total Power Consumption by Servers in the U.S. and the World," Stanford University, February 15, 2007; Brad Allenby and Darian Unger, "Information Technology Impacts on the U.S. Energy Demand Profile," proceedings of the E-Vision 2000 Conference, RAND Corporation, October 2000; Ted Balaker, "The Quiet Success: Telecommuting's Impact on Transportation and Beyond," Reason Foundation, October 2005; and Harri Andersson et al., "The Prospects for Graphic Paper: The Impact of Substitution, the Outlook for Demand," Boston Consulting Group, September 2007. Sightline also consulted the Semiconductor Industry Association, Flexcar, Commuter Challenge, and several media accounts, including those published in the *Hartford Courant*, *New Yorker* magazine, and the *New York Times*.

About the Author
and Sightline Institute

ERIC SORENSEN is a journalist with twenty-five years of daily newspaper experience, including five years as the science reporter for the *Seattle Times*. He holds an MS degree from the Columbia University Graduate School of Journalism, where he won the Ford Times Feature Writing Award. Sorensen is currently counting carbon in Kenmore, Washington, where he works as a freelance science writer and editor of the magazine *Pacific Yachting PNW*. He is a former program director of the Seattle nonprofit Resource Media and co-author of *Natural Wonders*, a book growing out of an award-winning *Seattle Times* series.

SIGHTLINE INSTITUTE (formerly Northwest Environment Watch), founded in 1993 by Alan Durning, is an independent nonprofit think tank based in Seattle. Its focus is Cascadia, or the Pacific Northwest, and its mission is to bring about sustainability—a healthy, lasting prosperity grounded in place. Sightline's only ideology is commitment to the shared values of community, responsibility, fairness, and opportunity.

Readers seeking more information about the organization or access to its other publications can visit Sightline's online resource center at *www.sightline.org*, which aims to make its research and tools widely accessible to engaged citizens. Visitors there can download books or reports, find compelling maps and graphics, and keep up with the latest sustainability news. Sightline welcomes feedback sent to *ask_us@sightline.org*.